1984

The American Film Institute

John F. Kennedy Center
for the Performing Arts
Washington, D.C. 20566

2021 North Western Avenue
P.O. Box 27999
Los Angeles, CA 90027

Editor: Thomas Wiener

Chief Researcher: Alice Leccese Powers

Editorial Assistant: Kathy Davis

Designer: Cynthia Friedman

Marketing Manager: Linda Miller

Publisher: Michael McCormick

Photographs courtesy of ABC-TV,
CBS-TV, Columbia Pictures, Metro-Goldwyn
Mayer, Museum of Modern Art/Film Stills,
NBC-TV, Paramount Pictures, Twentieth
Century-Fox, United Artists, Universal Pictures,
Warner Bros.

THE AMERICAN FILM INSTITUTE

The Kennedy Center, home of AFI's Washington offices.

The American Film Institute was established by the National Endowment for the Arts in 1967 as an independent, non-profit organization dedicated to preserving the heritage and advancing the art of film and television in America. Through a series of interrelated programs emanating from its offices in Washington, D.C. and its campus in Los Angeles, the institute conducts activities around the country that work toward the achievement of four primary goals:

☐ to increase recognition and understanding of the moving image as an art form;

☐ to assure preservation of the art form;

☐ to identify, develop, and encourage new talent;

☐ to establish, through innovative fundraising and sound fiscal management, the necessary resources for achievement of institute goals.

The main building of the AFI Campus in Los Angeles.

PROGRAMS OF THE INSTITUTE

PRESERVATION

Between the turn of the century and 1951, more than 21,000 feature-length films were produced in the United States. Only 50 percent survive today. For newsfilms, documentaries, and television programs, the survival rate is even less than half. Many of the motion pictures that survive are endangered: Nitrate theatrical films (pre-1950) decay into highly flammable brown powder; many color films fade to magenta; videotapes can deteriorate beyond recovery or may be deliberately erased.

In March of last year, the institute's Board of Trustees declared the years 1983-1993 as The Decade of Preservation, recognizing that by the motion picture's 100th birthday in 1993, the remaining nitrate film in this country most probably will have disappeared. Therefore, the trustees decided that a major 10-year campaign of fundraising and consciousness-raising could be initiated at no better time.

Currently, The American Film Institute Collection at the Library of Congress contains some 18,000 films that are being preserved for future generations. The institute's Preservation program also administers National Endowment for the Arts funds to film archives around the country, and it is in conjunction with them that the various major events and screenings planned for the next 10 years will occur.

The Louis B. Mayer Library, located in its own building at the Los Angeles campus, is one of the nation's leading research libraries specializing in film and television. With more than 5,000 books, 2,500 unpublished screenplays, and 130 regularly received periodicals, the library serves students, academicians, film historians, members of the professional film and television community, and individuals interested in film or television. The library's holdings include the personal papers and manuscripts of leading film figures as well as collections of important still photographs, transcripts of Master's Seminars at the Center for Advanced Film Studies, oral history transcripts, and clipping files housed in the Charles K. Feldman Reading Room and the Ahmanson Special Collections Room.

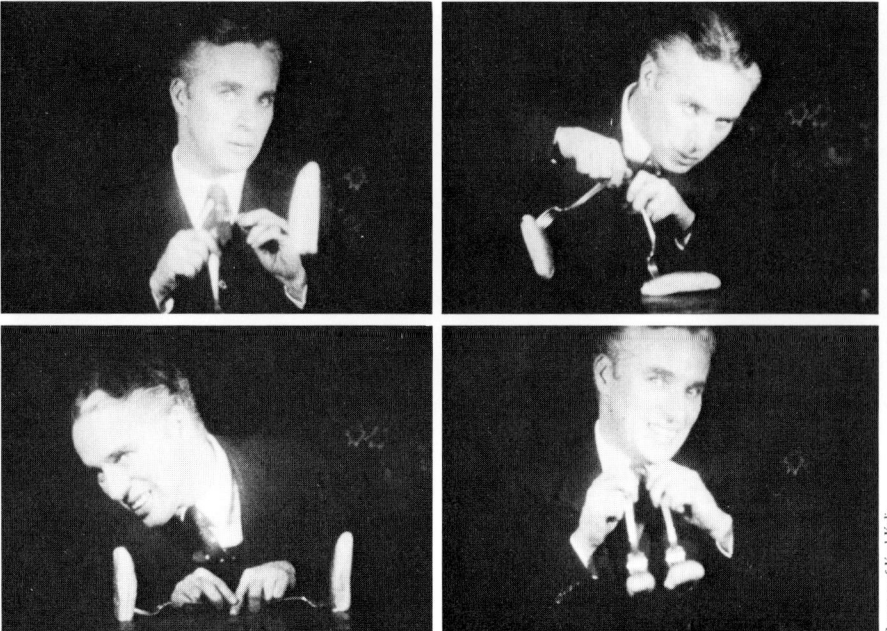

Charles Chaplin as "Gas House Mike" recreates the dance of the rolls from *The Gold Rush* in illustrator Ralph Barton's home movie version of *Camille*, co-written by Anita Loos.

AFI CATALOG

In 1983-84, with support from the National Endowment for the Humanities, the National Endowment for the Arts, and The David and Lucille Packard Foundation, the institute reactivated its Catalog Project. The project, which earlier completed and published information on films produced in the 1920s and 1960s, will next complete cataloging all feature films produced from 1911 through 1920, and will continue work on cataloging films produced from 1893 through 1910.

EXHIBITION

Screenings are one of the tools that the institute uses in fulfilling its mandate to increase recognition of the moving image as an art form. The institute's repertory theater in the Kennedy Center—The AFI Theater—screens 600-800 films a year in thematic series. Tours of film and video programs are presented at a variety of exhibition sites around the country. Both the AFI Theater in Washington and the Mark Goodson Screening Room at the Los Angeles campus are equipped with state-of-the-art video projection systems, providing a rare opportunity to view video in a theatrical setting.

LIFE ACHIEVEMENT AWARD

The Life Achievement Award is presented annually by the institute to honor an individual whose career achievement has "fundamentally advanced the art of American film and has withstood the test of time." Since its first presentation in 1973, the tribute has been telecast nationally by CBS and has been seen in 28 countries on five continents.

The honor, awarded by vote of the institute's Board of Trustees, has been presented to John Ford, James Cagney, Orson Welles, William Wyler, Bette Davis, Henry Fonda, Alfred Hitchcock, James Stewart, Fred Astaire, Frank Capra, and John Huston.

CENTER FOR ADVANCED FILM STUDIES

The institute's renowned conservatory for aspiring filmmakers, the Center for Advanced Film Studies, moved in 1981 to a new campus in Los Angeles that provides greatly expanded film and video production facilities including a state-of-the-art video production center, the Louis B. Mayer Library, classrooms, and screening rooms. There, the nation's most promising artists work under the guidance of, and in close association with, film and television's finest professionals. Fellows at the Center specialize in one of five areas: producing, directing, screenwriting, cinematography, or production design.

MEDIA PROGRAMS

Education, Production & Distribution
The Independent Filmmaker Program, funded by the National Endowment for the Arts and administered by the institute, annually awards grants to some of the nation's most promising video and filmmakers. The purpose of the program is to aid advanced artists in exploring new directions in their work. In cooperation with the NEA, the institute also launched a regional Independent Filmmaker Program, which is being administered by selected media arts centers. The regional program provides an important new avenue of assistance to aspiring video and film artists.

The institute's education liaison provides advice on curriculum development in film and television studies, responds to queries by students regarding film education and careers, and serves as a national catalyst for the encouragement and strengthening of film and television education in this country.

The Directing Workshop for Women provides professional women in the film and television industries with the opportunity to use their talents in directing narrative videotape projects. Divided into two-year cycles, the Directing Workshop for Women allows approximately 12 to 17 women the opportunity to direct up to two projects on videotape. From 1974 to September 1983, 66 women directed 92 projects through participation in the workshop.

Toward its goal of increasing recognition and understanding of the moving image as an art form, the institute sponsors lectures, seminars, conferences, courses, and workshops —primarily at its campus in Los Angeles. These activities deal with the practical and the intellectual aspects of the art form and are designed for both the general public and those professionally involved with the media arts.

TELEVISION AND VIDEO SERVICES

Television and Video Services sponsors conferences, workshops, and meetings for independent producers, the industry, community groups, and others interested in America's youngest media art form. Among the program's most important activities has been its annual National Video Festival, sponsored by the Sony Corporation. The festival, established in 1981, has become, in this short time, an important annual forum for artists working in video. Along with screenings, lectures, and discussions, the festival also includes a student competition that recognizes outstanding achievements in video production by young artists.

The program maintains a state-of-the-art center for all aspects of video production at the institute's Los Angeles campus with equipment provided by the Sony Corporation of America.

AMERICAN FILM

Since its first issue in 1975, *American Film* has grown in circulation and recognition to become the leading publication in the film and television field.

Published 10 times a year, *American Film* contains insightful articles on the film and television arts written by prominent filmmakers, authors, and critics. It regularly carries features about new film and television productions in progress, interviews with major film and television artists, reports on the impact of film and television on culture, reexaminations of classic films and their creators, and commentary on the emerging home video scene.

1984 HOLIDAYS

JANUARY
1   New Year's Day

FEBRUARY
12 Lincoln's Birthday
14 St. Valentine's Day
20 Washington's Birthday

MARCH
7   Ash Wednesday
17 St. Patrick's Day

APRIL
17 First Day of Passover
20 Good Friday
22 Easter

MAY
13 Mothers Day
28 Memorial Day

JUNE
14 Flag Day
17 Fathers Day

JULY
4   Independence Day

SEPTEMBER
3   Labor Day
27 Rosh Hashanah

OCTOBER
6   Yom Kippur
8   Columbus Day
31 Halloween

NOVEMBER
6   Election Day
11 Veterans Day
22 Thanksgiving

DECEMBER
19 First Day of Hanukkah
25 Christmas

1984

JANUARY
S	M	T	W	T	F	S
1	2	3	4	5	6	7
8	9	10	11	12	13	14
15	16	17	18	19	20	21
22	23	24	25	26	27	28
29	30	31				

FEBRUARY
S	M	T	W	T	F	S
			1	2	3	4
5	6	7	8	9	10	11
12	13	14	15	16	17	18
19	20	21	22	23	24	25
26	27	28	29			

MARCH
S	M	T	W	T	F	S
				1	2	3
4	5	6	7	8	9	10
11	12	13	14	15	16	17
18	19	20	21	22	23	24
25	26	27	28	29	30	31

APRIL
S	M	T	W	T	F	S
1	2	3	4	5	6	7
8	9	10	11	12	13	14
15	16	17	18	19	20	21
22	23	24	25	26	27	28
29	30					

MAY
S	M	T	W	T	F	S
		1	2	3	4	5
6	7	8	9	10	11	12
13	14	15	16	17	18	19
20	21	22	23	24	25	26
27	28	29	30	31		

JUNE
S	M	T	W	T	F	S
					1	2
3	4	5	6	7	8	9
10	11	12	13	14	15	16
17	18	19	20	21	22	23
24	25	26	27	28	29	30

JULY
S	M	T	W	T	F	S
1	2	3	4	5	6	7
8	9	10	11	12	13	14
15	16	17	18	19	20	21
22	23	24	25	26	27	28
29	30	31				

AUGUST
S	M	T	W	T	F	S
			1	2	3	4
5	6	7	8	9	10	11
12	13	14	15	16	17	18
19	20	21	22	23	24	25
26	27	28	29	30	31	

SEPTEMBER
S	M	T	W	T	F	S
						1
2	3	4	5	6	7	8
9	10	11	12	13	14	15
16	17	18	19	20	21	22
23	24	25	26	27	28	29
30						

OCTOBER
S	M	T	W	T	F	S
	1	2	3	4	5	6
7	8	9	10	11	12	13
14	15	16	17	18	19	20
21	22	23	24	25	26	27
28	29	30	31			

NOVEMBER
S	M	T	W	T	F	S
				1	2	3
4	5	6	7	8	9	10
11	12	13	14	15	16	17
18	19	20	21	22	23	24
25	26	27	28	29	30	

DECEMBER
S	M	T	W	T	F	S
						1
2	3	4	5	6	7	8
9	10	11	12	13	14	15
16	17	18	19	20	21	22
23	24	25	26	27	28	29
30	31					

JANUARY

S	M	T	W	T	F	S
1	2	3	4	5	6	7
8	9	10	11	12	13	14
15	16	17	18	19	20	21
22	23	24	25	26	27	28
29	30	31				

Paul Newman born, January 26, 1925 (*Cool Hand Luke*)

December / January

MONDAY 26	TUESDAY 27	WEDNESDAY 28	THURSDAY 29
Steve Allen born, 1921	Radio City Music Hall opens, 1932	F.W. Murnau born, 1888	
8:00	8:00	8:00	8:00
9:00	9:00	9:00	9:00
10:00	10:00	10:00	10:00
11:00	11:00	11:00	11:00
Noon	Noon	Noon	Noon
1:00	1:00	1:00	1:00
2:00	2:00	2:00	2:00
3:00	3:00	3:00	3:00
4:00	4:00	4:00	4:00
5:00	5:00	5:00	5:00
6:00	6:00	6:00	6:00
7:00	7:00	7:00	7:00

FRIDAY	SATURDAY
30	*31*
	Orry-Kelly born, 1897

8:00	
9:00	
10:00	
11:00	
Noon	
1:00	**SUNDAY**
	1
2:00	
3:00	**New Year's Day**
	First public showing of
	The Birth of a Nation, 1915
4:00	
5:00	
6:00	
7:00	

F.W. Murnau born, December 28, 1888 (*Sunrise*, with Janet Gaynor, George O'Brien)

DECEMBER							JANUARY							FEBRUARY						
S	M	T	W	T	F	S	S	M	T	W	T	F	S	S	M	T	W	T	F	S
				1	2	3	1	2	3	4	5	6	7				1	2	3	4
4	5	6	7	8	9	10	8	9	10	11	12	13	14	5	6	7	8	9	10	11
11	12	13	14	15	16	17	15	16	17	18	19	20	21	12	13	14	15	16	17	18
18	19	20	21	22	23	24	22	23	24	25	26	27	28	19	20	21	22	23	24	25
25	26	27	28	29	30	31	29	30	31					26	27	28	29			

JANUARY

MONDAY 2	TUESDAY 3	WEDNESDAY 4	THURSDAY 5
	Dorothy Arzner born, 1900 First telecast of "Dragnet," 1952	Dyan Cannon born, 1939	Robert Duvall born, 1931
8:00	8:00	8:00	8:00
9:00	9:00	9:00	9:00
10:00	10:00	10:00	10:00
11:00	11:00	11:00	11:00
Noon	Noon	Noon	Noon
1:00	1:00	1:00	1:00
2:00	2:00	2:00	2:00
3:00	3:00	3:00	3:00
4:00	4:00	4:00	4:00
5:00	5:00	5:00	5:00
6:00	6:00	6:00	6:00
7:00	7:00	7:00	7:00

FRIDAY
6

Danny Thomas born, 1914

8:00

9:00

10:00

11:00

Noon

1:00

2:00

3:00

4:00

5:00

6:00

7:00

SUGAR
8:30 BABIES

SATURDAY
7

Adolph Zukor born, 1873

SUNDAY
8

Elvis Presley born, 1935

Dyan Cannon born, January 4, 1939 (*Heaven Can Wait*, with Charles Grodin)

JANUARY

MONDAY 9	TUESDAY 10	WEDNESDAY 11	THURSDAY 12
	Sal Mineo born, 1939	Founders of the Academy of Motion Picture Arts and Sciences gather for first time, 1927	First and only screening of nine-hour, forty-two-minute version of *Greed*, 1924
Little Caesar opens, 1931 First telecast of "Rawhide," 1959	Walter Hill born, 1942 First telecast of "That Was the Week That Was," 1964	*Sons of the Desert* opens, 1934	
8:00	8:00	8:00	8:00
9:00	9:00	9:00	9:00
10:00	10:00	10:00	10:00
11:00	11:00	11:00	11:00
Noon	Noon	Noon	Noon
1:00	1:00	1:00	1:00
2:00	2:00	2:00	2:00
3:00	3:00	3:00	3:00
4:00	4:00	4:00	4:00
5:00	5:00	5:00	5:00
6:00	6:00	6:00	6:00
7:00	7:00	7:00	7:00

FRIDAY
13

Snow White and the Seven Dwarfs
opens, 1938

8:00

9:00

10:00

11:00

Noon

1:00

2:00

3:00

4:00

5:00

6:00

7:00

SATURDAY
14

Hal Roach born, 1892

Cecil Beaton born, 1904

Joseph Losey born, 1909

SUNDAY
15

First telecast of "Happy Days," 1974

Sons of the Desert opens, January 11, 1934 (Oliver Hardy, Stan Laurel)

DECEMBER						
S	M	T	W	T	F	S
					1	2	3
4	5	6	7	8	9	10
11	12	13	14	15	16	17
18	19	20	21	22	23	24
25	26	27	28	29	30	31

JANUARY						
S	M	T	W	T	F	S
1	2	3	4	5	6	7
8	9	10	11	12	13	14
15	16	17	18	19	20	21
22	23	24	25	26	27	28
29	30	31				

FEBRUARY						
S	M	T	W	T	F	S
				1	2	3	4
5	6	7	8	9	10	11
12	13	14	15	16	17	18
19	20	21	22	23	24	25
26	27	28	29			

JANUARY

MONDAY 16	TUESDAY 17	WEDNESDAY 18	THURSDAY 19
Harry Carey born, 1892 Ethel Merman born, 1908	Mack Sennett born, 1880 James Earl Jones born, 1931	Oliver Hardy born, 1892 Cary Grant born, 1904	Richard Lester born, 1932 *Miracle of Morgan's Creek* opens, 1944
8:00	8:00	8:00	8:00
9:00	9:00	9:00	9:00
10:00	10:00	10:00	10:00
11:00	11:00	11:00	11:00
Noon	Noon	Noon	Noon
1:00	1:00	1:00	1:00
2:00	2:00	2:00	2:00
3:00	3:00	3:00	3:00
4:00	4:00	4:00	4:00
5:00	5:00	5:00	5:00
6:00	6:00	6:00	6:00
7:00	7:00	7:00	7:00

FRIDAY
20

Frederico Fellini born, 1920
Patricia Neal born, 1926

8:00

9:00

10:00

11:00

Noon

1:00

2:00

3:00

4:00

5:00

6:00

7:00

SATURDAY
21

SUNDAY
22

D.W. Griffith born, 1875

James Earl Jones born, January 17, 1931

DECEMBER						
S	M	T	W	T	F	S
					1	2	3
4	5	6	7	8	9	10
11	12	13	14	15	16	17
18	19	20	21	22	23	24
25	26	27	28	29	30	31

JANUARY						
S	M	T	W	T	F	S
1	2	3	4	5	6	7
8	9	10	11	12	13	14
15	16	17	18	19	20	21
22	23	24	25	26	27	28
29	30	31				

FEBRUARY						
S	M	T	W	T	F	S
			1	2	3	4
5	6	7	8	9	10	11
12	13	14	15	16	17	18
19	20	21	22	23	24	25
26	27	28	29			

JANUARY

MONDAY 23	TUESDAY 24	WEDNESDAY 25	THURSDAY 26
Sergei Eisenstein born, 1898 Ernie Kovacs born, 1919 Rutger Hauer born, 1944	Ava Gardner born, 1922 George Cukor dies, 1983	First Emmy Awards presented, 1949	Paul Newman born, 1925
8:00	8:00	8:00	8:00
9:00	9:00	9:00	9:00
10:00	10:00	10:00	10:00
11:00	11:00	11:00	11:00
Noon	Noon	Noon	Noon
1:00	1:00	1:00	1:00
2:00	2:00	2:00	2:00
3:00	3:00	3:00	3:00
4:00	4:00	4:00	4:00
5:00	5:00	5:00	5:00
6:00	6:00	6:00	6:00
7:00	7:00	7:00	7:00

FRIDAY
27

Donna Reed born, 1921

First public demonstration of
television, by John L. Baird, 1926

8:00	
9:00	
10:00	
11:00	
Noon	
1:00	
2:00	
3:00	
4:00	
5:00	
6:00	
7:00	

SATURDAY
28

**Golden Globe Awards
New York Independent Film
Makers Exposition** (through
January 29)

SUNDAY
29

New York Film Critics Awards

Ava Gardner born, January 24, 1922 (*The Barefoot Contessa*, with
Humphrey Bogart)

DECEMBER								JANUARY								FEBRUARY						
S	M	T	W	T	F	S		S	M	T	W	T	F	S		S	M	T	W	T	F	S
					1	2	3		1	2	3	4	5	6	7					1	2	3	4
4	5	6	7	8	9	10		8	9	10	11	12	13	14		5	6	7	8	9	10	11
11	12	13	14	15	16	17		15	16	17	18	19	20	21		12	13	14	15	16	17	18
18	19	20	21	22	23	24		22	23	24	25	26	27	28		19	20	21	22	23	24	25
25	26	27	28	29	30	31		29	30	31						26	27	28	29			

MONDAY *30*	TUESDAY *31*	WEDNESDAY *1*	THURSDAY *2*
		First film studio, Edison's Black Maria, completed, 1893 John Ford born, 1895 S.J. Perelman born, 1904	
Gene Hackman born, 1931 *Dr. Strangelove* opens, 1964	Tallulah Bankhead born, 1903		
8:00	8:00	8:00	8:00
9:00	9:00	9:00	9:00
10:00	10:00	10:00	10:00
11:00	11:00	11:00	11:00
Noon	Noon	Noon	Noon
1:00	1:00	1:00	1:00
2:00	2:00	2:00	2:00
3:00	3:00	3:00	3:00
4:00	4:00	4:00	4:00
5:00	5:00	5:00	5:00
6:00	6:00	6:00	6:00
7:00	7:00	7:00	7:00

FRIDAY	SATURDAY
3	**4**
	Ida Lupino born, 1918

8:00	
9:00	
10:00	
11:00	
Noon	
1:00	**SUNDAY**
2:00	**5**
3:00	United Artists formed by Douglas Fairbanks, Mary Pickford, Charles Chaplin, and D.W. Griffith, 1919
4:00	
5:00	
6:00	
7:00	

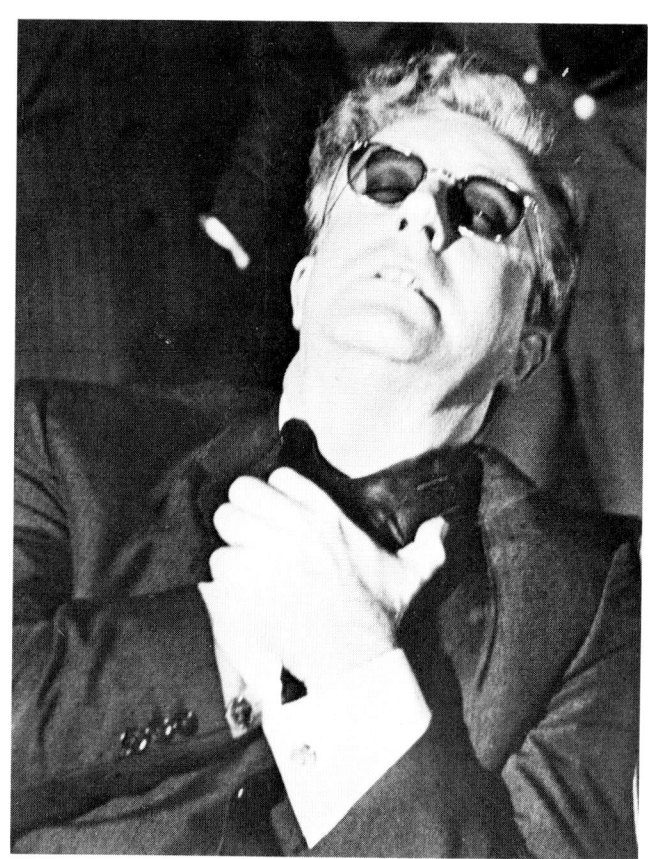

Dr. Strangelove opens, January 30, 1964 (Peter Sellers)

DECEMBER							JANUARY							FEBRUARY						
S	M	T	W	T	F	S	S	M	T	W	T	F	S	S	M	T	W	T	F	S
					1	2														
						3	1	2	3	4	5	6	7					1	2	3	4
4	5	6	7	8	9	10	8	9	10	11	12	13	14	5	6	7	8	9	10	11
11	12	13	14	15	16	17	15	16	17	18	19	20	21	12	13	14	15	16	17	18
18	19	20	21	22	23	24	22	23	24	25	26	27	28	19	20	21	22	23	24	25
25	26	27	28	29	30	31	29	30	31					26	27	28	29			

FEBRUARY

S	M	T	W	T	F	S
			1	2	3	4
5	6	7	8	9	10	11
12	13	14	15	16	17	18
19	20	21	22	23	24	25
26	27	28	29			

Bette Davis wins Oscar for performance in *Jezebel*, February 23, 1939

FEBRUARY

MONDAY 6	TUESDAY 7	WEDNESDAY 8	THURSDAY 9
		King Vidor born, 1984	
		Jack Lemmon born, 1925	
Ronald Reagan born, 1911		James Dean born, 1931	
François Truffaut born, 1932	Buster Crabbe born, 1907		Mia Farrow born, 1945
8:00	8:00	8:00	8:00
9:00	9:00	9:00	9:00
10:00	10:00	10:00	10:00
11:00	11:00	11:00	11:00
Noon	Noon	Noon	Noon
1:00	1:00	1:00	1:00
2:00	2:00	2:00	2:00
3:00	3:00	3:00	3:00
4:00	4:00	4:00	4:00
5:00	5:00	5:00	5:00
6:00	6:00	6:00	6:00
7:00	7:00	7:00	7:00

FRIDAY
10

**National Association of
Television Programming
Executives Conference, San
Francisco** (through February 14)

8:00	
9:00	
10:00	
11:00	
Noon	
1:00	
2:00	
3:00	
4:00	
5:00	
6:00	
7:00	

SATURDAY
11

Thomas Edison born, 1847

"Omnibus" wins Emmy for Best
Variety Program, 1954

SUNDAY
12

Lincoln's Birthday
Franco Zeffirelli born, 1922

King Vidor born, February 8, 1894 (with unidentified cameraman)

JANUARY

S	M	T	W	T	F	S
1	2	3	4	5	6	7
8	9	10	11	12	13	14
15	16	17	18	19	20	21
22	23	24	25	26	27	28
29	30	31				

FEBRUARY

S	M	T	W	T	F	S
			1	2	3	4
5	6	7	8	9	10	11
12	13	14	15	16	17	18
19	20	21	22	23	24	25
26	27	28	29			

MARCH

S	M	T	W	T	F	S
				1	2	3
4	5	6	7	8	9	10
11	12	13	14	15	16	17
18	19	20	21	22	23	24
25	26	27	28	29	30	31

FEBRUARY

MONDAY 13	TUESDAY 14	WEDNESDAY 15	THURSDAY 16
George Segal born, 1934 *Cabaret* opens, 1972	**Valentine's Day** Jack Benny born, 1894	John Barrymore born, 1882	Robert Flaherty born, 1884
8:00	8:00	8:00	8:00
9:00	9:00	9:00	9:00
10:00	10:00	10:00	10:00
11:00	11:00	11:00	11:00
Noon	Noon	Noon	Noon
1:00	1:00	1:00	1:00
2:00	2:00	2:00	2:00
3:00	3:00	3:00	3:00
4:00	4:00	4:00	4:00
5:00	5:00	5:00	5:00
6:00	6:00	6:00	6:00
7:00	7:00	7:00	7:00

FRIDAY	SATURDAY
17	*18*
	Milos Forman born, 1932
	John Travolta born, 1954
Alan Bates born, 1934	

8:00

9:00

10:00

11:00

Noon

	SUNDAY
1:00	*19*

2:00

3:00	Lee Marvin born, 1924
	John Frankenheimer born, 1930
	Seven Days in May opens, 1964

4:00

5:00

6:00

7:00

John Barrymore born, February 15, 1882 (*Don Juan*, with Mary Astor)

JANUARY

S	M	T	W	T	F	S
1	2	3	4	5	6	7
8	9	10	11	12	13	14
15	16	17	18	19	20	21
22	23	24	25	26	27	28
29	30	31				

FEBRUARY

S	M	T	W	T	F	S
			1	2	3	4
5	6	7	8	9	10	11
12	13	14	15	16	17	18
19	20	21	22	23	24	25
26	27	28	29			

MARCH

S	M	T	W	T	F	S
				1	2	3
4	5	6	7	8	9	10
11	12	13	14	15	16	17
18	19	20	21	22	23	24
25	26	27	28	29	30	31

FEBRUARY

MONDAY 20	TUESDAY 21	WEDNESDAY 22	THURSDAY 23
Washington's Birthday Sidney Poitier born, 1924 *The African Queen* opens, 1952	Sam Peckinpah born, 1925	Luis Buñuel born, 1900 Giuletta Masina born, 1920	Bette Davis wins Oscar for performance in *Jezebel*, 1939 Peter Fonda born, 1939
8:00	8:00	8:00	8:00
9:00	9:00	9:00	9:00
10:00	10:00	10:00	10:00
11:00	11:00	11:00	11:00
Noon	Noon	Noon	Noon
1:00	1:00	1:00	1:00
2:00	2:00	2:00	2:00
3:00	3:00	3:00	3:00
4:00	4:00	4:00	4:00
5:00	5:00	5:00	5:00
6:00	6:00	6:00	6:00
7:00	7:00	7:00	7:00

FRIDAY	SATURDAY
24	**25**
Marjorie Main born, 1890	
Michel Legrand born, 1931	Tennessee Williams dies, 1983

8:00

9:00

10:00

11:00

Noon

1:00

<table>
<tr><td>2:00</td><td>SUNDAY</td></tr>
</table>

26

First public demonstration of
Kinemacolor, 1909

3:00

4:00

5:00

6:00

7:00

The African Queen opens, February 20, 1952 (Humphrey Bogart,
Katharine Hepburn)

JANUARY

S	M	T	W	T	F	S
1	2	3	4	5	6	7
8	9	10	11	12	13	14
15	16	17	18	19	20	21
22	23	24	25	26	27	28
29	30	31				

FEBRUARY

S	M	T	W	T	F	S
			1	2	3	4
5	6	7	8	9	10	11
12	13	14	15	16	17	18
19	20	21	22	23	24	25
26	27	28	29			

MARCH

S	M	T	W	T	F	S
				1	2	3
4	5	6	7	8	9	10
11	12	13	14	15	16	17
18	19	20	21	22	23	24
25	26	27	28	29	30	31

FEBRUARY / MARCH

MONDAY 27	TUESDAY 28	WEDNESDAY 29	THURSDAY 1
	Ben Hecht born, 1893 Marcel Pagnol born, 1893 Last episode of "M*A*S*H" draws record ratings, 1983		First official national network index report, by A.C. Nielsen Co., 1950
Elizabeth Taylor born, 1932		Michele Morgan born, 1920	
8:00	8:00	8:00	8:00
9:00	9:00	9:00	9:00
10:00	10:00	10:00	10:00
11:00	11:00	11:00	11:00
Noon	Noon	Noon	Noon
1:00	1:00	1:00	1:00
2:00	2:00	2:00	2:00
3:00	3:00	3:00	3:00
4:00	4:00	4:00	4:00
5:00	5:00	5:00	5:00
6:00	6:00	6:00	6:00
7:00	7:00	7:00	7:00

FRIDAY
2

Stagecoach opens, 1939

Casablanca wins Oscar for Best
Picture, 1944

8:00

9:00

10:00

11:00

Noon

1:00

2:00

3:00

4:00

5:00

6:00

7:00

SATURDAY
3

Jean Harlow born, 1911

SUNDAY
4

John Ford wins first Oscar, for *The
Informer*, 1936

Elizabeth Taylor born, February 27, 1932 (*A Date with Judy*,
with Jane Powell)

JANUARY

S	M	T	W	T	F	S
1	2	3	4	5	6	7
8	9	10	11	12	13	14
15	16	17	18	19	20	21
22	23	24	25	26	27	28
29	30	31				

FEBRUARY

S	M	T	W	T	F	S
			1	2	3	4
5	6	7	8	9	10	11
12	13	14	15	16	17	18
19	20	21	22	23	24	25
26	27	28	29			

MARCH

S	M	T	W	T	F	S
				1	2	3
4	5	6	7	8	9	10
11	12	13	14	15	16	17
18	19	20	21	22	23	24
25	26	27	28	29	30	31

MARCH

S	M	T	W	T	F	S
				1	2	3
4	5	6	7	8	9	10
11	12	13	14	15	16	17
18	19	20	21	22	23	24
25	26	27	28	29	30	31

Steve McQueen born, March 24, 1930 (*The Sand Pebbles*)

GO BEHIND THE SCENES

This is your invitation to go behind the scenes of the world's greatest motion picture and television productions; to learn how excellence comes to the screen; and to help preserve the heritage and advance the art of the moving image in America.

As a member of The American Film Institute, you'll enjoy *American Film* magazine and many other opportunities to help you better understand and appreciate the creative accomplishments of fine motion pictures and television. Your viewing will be more perceptive and enjoyable because you'll know the stories behind the ones shown on the screen.

Each issue of *American Film* takes you to the sets and studios for glimpses of work in production. You'll read about new movies and TV shows in the making, hear from their creators, explore classics of the past, and keep up-to-date on fast moving developments in home video.

But *American Film* is just one way the institute acts on your behalf to stimulate the kind of films that enrich the quality of our lives. Your membership helps support other worthwhile institute activities, among them programs that preserve and exhibit classic films, and that encourage new talent through grants and through the AFI Center for Advanced Film Studies in Los Angeles.

For an annual fee of just $20 you can join over 120,000 AFI members who share a special commitment to the art of the moving image. Use the attached order form to join today!

Orson Welles on the set of *Citizen Kane.*

Exclusive AFI Member Privileges:

★ ***American Film* Magazine**—receive ten issues annually of the world's favorite magazine on film and television . . . lively, colorful, informative coverage

★ **Movie Ticket Discounts**—save on admission to classic, feature, and independent films, as well as selected film festivals

★ **Museum Admission Discounts**—pay member's price at selected museums

★ **Courses, Lectures, Special Events**—attend these AFI-sponsored programs at substantial member savings

★ **Books, Videotapes, Merchandise**—our special selection of quality items at special member prices

★ **Many Other Privileges**—car rental discounts, key chain registration service, use of AFI library collections, and more!

★ **Personal Membership Card**—identifies you worldwide as a patron of the film and video arts

---

Join The American Film Institute
One Year for $20|With A Special "No Risk" Guarantee

I accept your invitation to become a member of The American Film Institute. I understand that my $20 membership dues entitle me to 10 issues (1 year) of *American Film* magazine, and other valuable member benefits and privileges, for the single-copy price of the magazine alone.

☐ $20 Dues Enclosed   ☐ Bill Me   ☐ Outside USA, $27

Name_____

Address_____ Apt. No._____

City_____

State_____ Zip_____

If at any time, for any reason, you are less than completely satisfied, we will refund your *entire* dues payment—regardless of how many months you have been a member.

The American Film Institute is a not-for-profit corporation with a 501-C-3 designation. Annual dues may be deductible, as provided by law.

American Film Brings the Movies Home.

 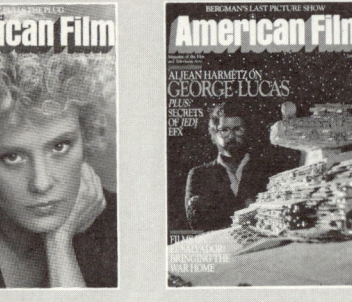   

**A subscription to the world's most widely-read film
and television magazine is just one benefit of membership in
The American Film Institute.**

MARCH

MONDAY 5	TUESDAY 6	WEDNESDAY 7	THURSDAY 8
		Ash Wednesday	
	First television broadcast from an airplane in flight, 1940	Anna Magnani born, 1908 Emmy Awards first telecast, 1955	Lynn Redgrave born, 1943
8:00	8:00	8:00	8:00
9:00	9:00	9:00	9:00
10:00	10:00	10:00	10:00
11:00	11:00	11:00	11:00
Noon	Noon	Noon	Noon
1:00	1:00	1:00	1:00
2:00	2:00	2:00	2:00
3:00	3:00	3:00	3:00
4:00	4:00	4:00	4:00
5:00	5:00	5:00	5:00
6:00	6:00	6:00	6:00
7:00	7:00	7:00	7:00

FRIDAY
9

Edward R. Murrow denounces Joseph McCarthy on "See It Now," 1954

SATURDAY
10

Directors Guild of America Awards

First film shot in California, D.W. Griffith's *In Old California*, released, 1910

8:00	
9:00	
10:00	
11:00	
Noon	
1:00	
2:00	
3:00	
4:00	
5:00	
6:00	
7:00	

SUNDAY
11

The Roxy, largest movie theater ever built, opens, 1927

Anna Magnani born, March 7, 1908

FEBRUARY

S	M	T	W	T	F	S
			1	2	3	4
5	6	7	8	9	10	11
12	13	14	15	16	17	18
19	20	21	22	23	24	25
26	27	28	29			

MARCH

S	M	T	W	T	F	S
				1	2	3
4	5	6	7	8	9	10
11	12	13	14	15	16	17
18	19	20	21	22	23	24
25	26	27	28	29	30	31

APRIL

S	M	T	W	T	F	S
1	2	3	4	5	6	7
8	9	10	11	12	13	14
15	16	17	18	19	20	21
22	23	24	25	26	27	28
29	30					

MARCH

MONDAY *12*	TUESDAY *13*	WEDNESDAY *14*	THURSDAY *15*
			Universal City opens, 1915 *The Godfather* opens, 1972
Beat the Devil opens, 1954		Michael Caine born, 1933	
8:00	8:00	8:00	8:00
9:00	9:00	9:00	9:00
10:00	10:00	10:00	10:00
11:00	11:00	11:00	11:00
Noon	Noon	Noon	Noon
1:00	1:00	1:00	1:00
2:00	2:00	2:00	2:00
3:00	3:00	3:00	3:00
4:00	4:00	4:00	4:00
5:00	5:00	5:00	5:00
6:00	6:00	6:00	6:00
7:00	7:00	7:00	7:00

FRIDAY
16

Katharine Hepburn wins first of four Oscars, for *Morning Glory*, 1934

Arthur Godfrey dies, 1983

8:00

9:00

10:00

11:00

Noon

1:00

2:00

3:00

4:00

5:00

6:00

7:00

SATURDAY
17

St. Patrick's Day

SUNDAY
18

The Diary of Anne Frank opens, 1959

Rio Bravo opens, 1959

Arthur Godfrey dies, March 16, 1983

FEBRUARY						
S	M	T	W	T	F	S
				1	2	3	4
5	6	7	8	9	10	11
12	13	14	15	16	17	18
19	20	21	22	23	24	25
26	27	28	29			

MARCH						
S	M	T	W	T	F	S
					1	2	3
4	5	6	7	8	9	10
11	12	13	14	15	16	17
18	19	20	21	22	23	24
25	26	27	28	29	30	31

APRIL						
S	M	T	W	T	F	S
1	2	3	4	5	6	7
8	9	10	11	12	13	14
15	16	17	18	19	20	21
22	23	24	25	26	27	28
29	30					

MARCH

MONDAY *19*	TUESDAY *20*	WEDNESDAY *21*	THURSDAY *22*
	First experimental color television program airs, 1941 *Blackboard Jungle* opens, 1955		
Academy Awards telecast for the first time, 1953		Broncho Billy Anderson born, 1882	Lumiere brothers present their first film, 1913
8:00	8:00	8:00	8:00
9:00	9:00	9:00	9:00
10:00	10:00	10:00	10:00
11:00	11:00	11:00	11:00
Noon	Noon	Noon	Noon
1:00	1:00	1:00	1:00
2:00	2:00	2:00	2:00
3:00	3:00	3:00	3:00
4:00	4:00	4:00	4:00
5:00	5:00	5:00	5:00
6:00	6:00	6:00	6:00
7:00	7:00	7:00	7:00

FRIDAY
23

Joan Crawford born, 1904
Akira Kurosawa born, 1910

8:00	
9:00	
10:00	
11:00	
Noon	
1:00	
2:00	
3:00	
4:00	
5:00	
6:00	
7:00	

SATURDAY
24

Steve McQueen born, 1930
John Huston and Walter Huston win
Oscars for *The Treasure of the
Sierra Madre*, 1949

SUNDAY
25

David Lean born, 1908
Fred Zinnemann wins Oscar for
From Here to Eternity, 1954

Joan Crawford born, March 23, 1904 (*Dancing Lady*, with Clark Gable)

FEBRUARY
S	M	T	W	T	F	S
			1	2	3	4
5	6	7	8	9	10	11
12	13	14	15	16	17	18
19	20	21	22	23	24	25
26	27	28	29			

MARCH
S	M	T	W	T	F	S
				1	2	3
4	5	6	7	8	9	10
11	12	13	14	15	16	17
18	19	20	21	22	23	24
25	26	27	28	29	30	31

APRIL
S	M	T	W	T	F	S
1	2	3	4	5	6	7
8	9	10	11	12	13	14
15	16	17	18	19	20	21
22	23	24	25	26	27	28
29	30					

MARCH / APRIL

MONDAY 26	TUESDAY 27	WEDNESDAY 28	THURSDAY 29
			Society for Cinema Studies Annual Conference, Madison, Wisconsin (through April 1) *Some Like It Hot* opens, 1959
Alan Arkin born, 1934 James Caan born, 1939	Gloria Swanson born, 1897	Pandro S. Berman born, 1925	
8:00	8:00	8:00	8:00
9:00	9:00	9:00	9:00
10:00	10:00	10:00	10:00
11:00	11:00	11:00	11:00
Noon	Noon	Noon	Noon
1:00	1:00	1:00	1:00
2:00	2:00	2:00	2:00
3:00	3:00	3:00	3:00
4:00	4:00	4:00	4:00
5:00	5:00	5:00	5:00
6:00	6:00	6:00	6:00
7:00	7:00	7:00	7:00

FRIDAY
30

Warren Beatty born, 1937

SATURDAY
31

Motion Picture Producers and Distributors Association enacts Production Code, 1930

8:00

9:00

10:00

11:00

Noon

1:00

SUNDAY
1

2:00

3:00

Toshiro Mifune born, 1920

Debbie Reynolds born, 1932

4:00

5:00

6:00

7:00

Alan Arkin born, March 26, 1934; James Caan born, March 26, 1939 (*Freebie and the Bean*)

<table>
<tr><td colspan="7">FEBRUARY</td></tr>
<tr><td>S</td><td>M</td><td>T</td><td>W</td><td>T</td><td>F</td><td>S</td></tr>
<tr><td></td><td></td><td></td><td>1</td><td>2</td><td>3</td><td>4</td></tr>
<tr><td>5</td><td>6</td><td>7</td><td>8</td><td>9</td><td>10</td><td>11</td></tr>
<tr><td>12</td><td>13</td><td>14</td><td>15</td><td>16</td><td>17</td><td>18</td></tr>
<tr><td>19</td><td>20</td><td>21</td><td>22</td><td>23</td><td>24</td><td>25</td></tr>
<tr><td>26</td><td>27</td><td>28</td><td>29</td><td></td><td></td><td></td></tr>
</table>

<table>
<tr><td colspan="7">MARCH</td></tr>
<tr><td>S</td><td>M</td><td>T</td><td>W</td><td>T</td><td>F</td><td>S</td></tr>
<tr><td></td><td></td><td></td><td></td><td>1</td><td>2</td><td>3</td></tr>
<tr><td>4</td><td>5</td><td>6</td><td>7</td><td>8</td><td>9</td><td>10</td></tr>
<tr><td>11</td><td>12</td><td>13</td><td>14</td><td>15</td><td>16</td><td>17</td></tr>
<tr><td>18</td><td>19</td><td>20</td><td>21</td><td>22</td><td>23</td><td>24</td></tr>
<tr><td>25</td><td>26</td><td>27</td><td>28</td><td>29</td><td>30</td><td>31</td></tr>
</table>

<table>
<tr><td colspan="7">APRIL</td></tr>
<tr><td>S</td><td>M</td><td>T</td><td>W</td><td>T</td><td>F</td><td>S</td></tr>
<tr><td>1</td><td>2</td><td>3</td><td>4</td><td>5</td><td>6</td><td>7</td></tr>
<tr><td>8</td><td>9</td><td>10</td><td>11</td><td>12</td><td>13</td><td>14</td></tr>
<tr><td>15</td><td>16</td><td>17</td><td>18</td><td>19</td><td>20</td><td>21</td></tr>
<tr><td>22</td><td>23</td><td>24</td><td>25</td><td>26</td><td>27</td><td>28</td></tr>
<tr><td>29</td><td>30</td><td></td><td></td><td></td><td></td><td></td></tr>
</table>

APRIL

S	M	T	W	T	F	S
1	2	3	4	5	6	7
8	9	10	11	12	13	14
15	16	17	18	19	20	21
22	23	24	25	26	27	28
29	30					

Doris Day born, April 3, 1924

APRIL

MONDAY 2	TUESDAY 3	WEDNESDAY 4	THURSDAY 5
	Doris Day born, 1924 Marlon Brando born, 1924 *Broadway Melody* wins Oscar as Best Picture, 1929	FCC grants NBC permit for experimental television station, 1928 Gloria Swanson dies, 1983	**International Federation of Film Archives Annual Meeting, Vienna** (through April 11) Warner Bros. incorporated, 1923
First telecast of "Dallas", 1978			
8:00	8:00	8:00	8:00
9:00	9:00	9:00	9:00
10:00	10:00	10:00	10:00
11:00	11:00	11:00	11:00
Noon	Noon	Noon	Noon
1:00	1:00	1:00	1:00
2:00	2:00	2:00	2:00
3:00	3:00	3:00	3:00
4:00	4:00	4:00	4:00
5:00	5:00	5:00	5:00
6:00	6:00	6:00	6:00
7:00	7:00	7:00	7:00

FRIDAY
6

Walter Huston born, 1884

Dudley Nichols born, 1895

First motorized projector, the
Kinematograph, demonstrated,
1896

SATURDAY
7

Francis Ford Coppola born, 1939

8:00	
9:00	
10:00	
11:00	
Noon	
1:00	

SUNDAY
8

Andre Bazin born, 1918

2:00	
3:00	
4:00	
5:00	
6:00	
7:00	

First telecast of "Dallas," April 2, 1978 (Larry Hagman)

MARCH						
S	M	T	W	T	F	S
					1	2	3
4	5	6	7	8	9	10
11	12	13	14	15	16	17
18	19	20	21	22	23	24
25	26	27	28	29	30	31

APRIL						
S	M	T	W	T	F	S
1	2	3	4	5	6	7
8	9	10	11	12	13	14
15	16	17	18	19	20	21
22	23	24	25	26	27	28
29	30					

MAY						
S	M	T	W	T	F	S
		1	2	3	4	5
6	7	8	9	10	11	12
13	14	15	16	17	18	19
20	21	22	23	24	25	26
27	28	29	30	31		

APRIL

MONDAY 9	TUESDAY 10	WEDNESDAY 11	THURSDAY 12
First film archive established, at the Royal Library in Copenhagen, 1913	First telecast of NBC News, 1944	Norman McLaren born, 1914 Delores Del Rio dies, 1983	*Grand Hotel* opens, 1932
8:00	8:00	8:00	8:00
9:00	9:00	9:00	9:00
10:00	10:00	10:00	10:00
11:00	11:00	11:00	11:00
Noon	Noon	Noon	Noon
1:00	1:00	1:00	1:00
2:00	2:00	2:00	2:00
3:00	3:00	3:00	3:00
4:00	4:00	4:00	4:00
5:00	5:00	5:00	5:00
6:00	6:00	6:00	6:00
7:00	7:00	7:00	7:00

FRIDAY
13

Stanley Donen born, 1924

Melvyn Douglas wins Oscar for performance in *Hud*, 1964

8:00

9:00

10:00

11:00

Noon

1:00

2:00

3:00

4:00

5:00

6:00

7:00

SATURDAY
14

First Kinetoscope parlor opens, in New York, 1894

SUNDAY
15

First sound film screened before paying audience, Rialto Theatre, New York, 1923

Melvyn Douglas wins Oscar for performance in *Hud*, April 13, 1964 (with Paul Newman)

MARCH						
S	M	T	W	T	F	S
					1	2	3
4	5	6	7	8	9	10
11	12	13	14	15	16	17
18	19	20	21	22	23	24
25	26	27	28	29	30	31

APRIL						
S	M	T	W	T	F	S
1	2	3	4	5	6	7
8	9	10	11	12	13	14
15	16	17	18	19	20	21
22	23	24	25	26	27	28
29	30					

MAY						
S	M	T	W	T	F	S
			1	2	3	4	5
6	7	8	9	10	11	12
13	14	15	16	17	18	19
20	21	22	23	24	25	26
27	28	29	30	31		

APRIL

MONDAY 16	TUESDAY 17	WEDNESDAY 18	THURSDAY 19
	Passover		
	FCC rules that television must broadcast opposing views of controversial issues, 1950	Fatty Arbuckle banned from screen by MPDDA, 1922	ABC airs first network program, "On the Corner," 1948
Charlie Chaplin born, 1889			
8:00	8:00	8:00	8:00
9:00	9:00	9:00	9:00
10:00	10:00	10:00	10:00
11:00	11:00	11:00	11:00
Noon	Noon	Noon	Noon
1:00	1:00	1:00	1:00
2:00	2:00	2:00	2:00
3:00	3:00	3:00	3:00
4:00	4:00	4:00	4:00
5:00	5:00	5:00	5:00
6:00	6:00	6:00	6:00
7:00	7:00	7:00	7:00

FRIDAY
20

Good Friday

Western Electric and Warner Bros. form Vitaphone Co., 1926

8:00

9:00

10:00

11:00

Noon

1:00

2:00

3:00

4:00

5:00

6:00

7:00

SATURDAY
21

Edwin S. Porter born, 1869

Billy Bitzer born, 1872

Elaine May born, 1932

SUNDAY
22

Easter

Jack Nicholson born, 1937

Broadcast of Army-McCarthy hearings begins, 1954

Jack Nicholson born, April 22, 1937 (*The Last Detail*)

MARCH						
S	M	T	W	T	F	S
					1	2	3
4	5	6	7	8	9	10
11	12	13	14	15	16	17
18	19	20	21	22	23	24
25	26	27	28	29	30	31

APRIL						
S	M	T	W	T	F	S
1	2	3	4	5	6	7
8	9	10	11	12	13	14
15	16	17	18	19	20	21
22	23	24	25	26	27	28
29	30					

MAY						
S	M	T	W	T	F	S
			1	2	3	4	5
6	7	8	9	10	11	12
13	14	15	16	17	18	19
20	21	22	23	24	25	26
27	28	29	30	31		

APRIL

MONDAY 23	TUESDAY 24	WEDNESDAY 25	THURSDAY 26
	Leslie Howard born, 1893 Shirley MacLaine born, 1934		William Desmond Taylor born, 1877
The Pink Panther opens, 1964		Paul Mazursky born, 1930	Jean Vigo born, 1905
8:00	8:00	8:00	8:00
9:00	9:00	9:00	9:00
10:00	10:00	10:00	10:00
11:00	11:00	11:00	11:00
Noon	Noon	Noon	Noon
1:00	1:00	1:00	1:00
2:00	2:00	2:00	2:00
3:00	3:00	3:00	3:00
4:00	4:00	4:00	4:00
5:00	5:00	5:00	5:00
6:00	6:00	6:00	6:00
7:00	7:00	7:00	7:00

FRIDAY	SATURDAY
27	**28**
Broadcast Education Association Annual Convention, Las Vegas (through April 28)	
MIP Market, Cannes	*Bananas* opens, 1971

8:00	
9:00	
10:00	
11:00	
Noon	

1:00	SUNDAY
2:00	**29**
3:00	**National Association of Broadcasters Annual Convention, Las Vegas** (through May 2)
4:00	
5:00	
6:00	
7:00	

Leslie Howard born, April 24, 1893 (*The Petrified Forest*, with Bette Davis)

MARCH

S	M	T	W	T	F	S
					1	2	3
4	5	6	7	8	9	10
11	12	13	14	15	16	17
18	19	20	21	22	23	24
25	26	27	28	29	30	31

APRIL

S	M	T	W	T	F	S
1	2	3	4	5	6	7
8	9	10	11	12	13	14
15	16	17	18	19	20	21
22	23	24	25	26	27	28
29	30					

MAY

S	M	T	W	T	F	S
		1	2	3	4	5
6	7	8	9	10	11	12
13	14	15	16	17	18	19
20	21	22	23	24	25	26
27	28	29	30	31		

APRIL/MAY

MONDAY *30*	TUESDAY *1*	WEDNESDAY *2*	THURSDAY *3*
Fred MacMurray born, 1908 Jill Clayburgh born, 1944	*Citizen Kane* opens, 1941	*Going My Way* opens, 1944	First telecast of CBS News, 1948
8:00	8:00	8:00	8:00
9:00	9:00	9:00	9:00
10:00	10:00	10:00	10:00
11:00	11:00	11:00	11:00
Noon	Noon	Noon	Noon
1:00	1:00	1:00	1:00
2:00	2:00	2:00	2:00
3:00	3:00	3:00	3:00
4:00	4:00	4:00	4:00
5:00	5:00	5:00	5:00
6:00	6:00	6:00	6:00
7:00	7:00	7:00	7:00

FRIDAY
4

Audrey Hepburn born, 1929

8:00

9:00

10:00

11:00

Noon

1:00

2:00

3:00

4:00

5:00

6:00

7:00

SATURDAY
5

Tyrone Power born, 1913

SUNDAY
6

Max Ophuls born, 1902

Orson Welles born, 1915

Raymond Burr wins Emmy for "Perry Mason," 1959

Max Ophuls born, May 6, 1902 (*Letter From an Unknown Woman*, with George Macready, Joan Fontaine)

MARCH						
S	M	T	W	T	F	S
					1	2	3
4	5	6	7	8	9	10
11	12	13	14	15	16	17
18	19	20	21	22	23	24
25	26	27	28	29	30	31

APRIL						
S	M	T	W	T	F	S
1	2	3	4	5	6	7
8	9	10	11	12	13	14
15	16	17	18	19	20	21
22	23	24	25	26	27	28
29	30					

MAY						
S	M	T	W	T	F	S
			1	2	3	4	5
6	7	8	9	10	11	12
13	14	15	16	17	18	19
20	21	22	23	24	25	26
27	28	29	30	31		

MAY

S	M	T	W	T	F	S
		1	2	3	4	5
6	7	8	9	10	11	12
13	14	15	16	17	18	19
20	21	22	23	24	25	26
27	28	29	30	31		

Star Wars opens, May 25, 1977 (Harrison Ford)

MAY

MONDAY 7	TUESDAY 8	WEDNESDAY 9	THURSDAY 10
		Fay Kanin born, 1917	Max Steiner born, 1888
Gary Cooper born, 1901	Roberto Rossellini born, 1906	Albert Finney born, 1936	Fred Astaire born, 1899
8:00	8:00	8:00	8:00
9:00	9:00	9:00	9:00
10:00	10:00	10:00	10:00
11:00	11:00	11:00	11:00
Noon	Noon	Noon	Noon
1:00	1:00	1:00	1:00
2:00	2:00	2:00	2:00
3:00	3:00	3:00	3:00
4:00	4:00	4:00	4:00
5:00	5:00	5:00	5:00
6:00	6:00	6:00	6:00
7:00	7:00	7:00	7:00

FRIDAY
11

"Archie Bunker's Place" canceled
after 13 seasons (including years as
"All in the Family"), 1983

8:00

9:00

10:00

11:00

Noon

1:00

2:00

3:00

4:00

5:00

6:00

7:00

SATURDAY
12

SUNDAY
13

Mother's Day
Jack Valenti becomes president of
MPAA, 1966

Albert Finney born, May 9, 1936 (*Two for the Road*)

APRIL

S	M	T	W	T	F	S
1	2	3	4	5	6	7
8	9	10	11	12	13	14
15	16	17	18	19	20	21
22	23	24	25	26	27	28
29	30					

MAY

S	M	T	W	T	F	S
		1	2	3	4	5
6	7	8	9	10	11	12
13	14	15	16	17	18	19
20	21	22	23	24	25	26
27	28	29	30	31		

JUNE

S	M	T	W	T	F	S
					1	2
3	4	5	6	7	8	9
10	11	12	13	14	15	16
17	18	19	20	21	22	23
24	25	26	27	28	29	30

MAY

MONDAY 14	TUESDAY 15	WEDNESDAY 16	THURSDAY 17
	First double bill presented, Melbourne, Australia, 1911 Screen Actors Guild recognized as bargaining agent for actors, 1937	Henry Fonda born, 1905 Margaret Sullavan born, 1911 First Academy Awards ceremony, 1929	Metro Pictures, Goldwyn Pictures, and Louis B. Mayer form MGM, 1924
8:00	8:00	8:00	8:00
9:00	9:00	9:00	9:00
10:00	10:00	10:00	10:00
11:00	11:00	11:00	11:00
Noon	Noon	Noon	Noon
1:00	1:00	1:00	1:00
2:00	2:00	2:00	2:00
3:00	3:00	3:00	3:00
4:00	4:00	4:00	4:00
5:00	5:00	5:00	5:00
6:00	6:00	6:00	6:00
7:00	7:00	7:00	7:00

FRIDAY	SATURDAY
18	*19*

Little Miss Marker opens, 1934

8:00	
9:00	
10:00	
11:00	
Noon	
1:00	**SUNDAY**
	20
2:00	
3:00	First film screened before paying
	audience, *Young Griffo vs. Battling*
	Charles Bartlett, New York, 1895
4:00	
5:00	
6:00	
7:00	

Margaret Sullavan born, May 16, 1911 (*The Mortal Storm*, with James Stewart, Robert Young)

MAY

MONDAY 21	TUESDAY 22	WEDNESDAY 23	THURSDAY 24
	First public demonstration of motion pictures, Edison labs, 1891		
Robert Montgomery born, 1904	Laurence Olivier born, 1907	Douglas Fairbanks born, 1883	
8:00	8:00	8:00	8:00
9:00	9:00	9:00	9:00
10:00	10:00	10:00	10:00
11:00	11:00	11:00	11:00
Noon	Noon	Noon	Noon
1:00	1:00	1:00	1:00
2:00	2:00	2:00	2:00
3:00	3:00	3:00	3:00
4:00	4:00	4:00	4:00
5:00	5:00	5:00	5:00
6:00	6:00	6:00	6:00
7:00	7:00	7:00	7:00

FRIDAY
25

Star Wars opens, 1977

The Empire Strikes Back opens, 1980

The Return of the Jedi opens, 1983

8:00	
9:00	
10:00	
11:00	
Noon	
1:00	
2:00	
3:00	
4:00	
5:00	
6:00	
7:00	

SATURDAY
26

Al Jolson born, 1886

Henry Ephron born, 1912

First telecast of "The Dick Cavett Show," 1969

SUNDAY
27

Frank S. Nugent born, 1908

Robert Montgomery born, May 21, 1904 (*Fast and Loose*, with Rosalind Russell)

APRIL						
S	M	T	W	T	F	S
1	2	3	4	5	6	7
8	9	10	11	12	13	14
15	16	17	18	19	20	21
22	23	24	25	26	27	28
29	30					

MAY						
S	M	T	W	T	F	S
		1	2	3	4	5
6	7	8	9	10	11	12
13	14	15	16	17	18	19
20	21	22	23	24	25	26
27	28	29	30	31		

JUNE						
S	M	T	W	T	F	S
					1	2
3	4	5	6	7	8	9
10	11	12	13	14	15	16
17	18	19	20	21	22	23
24	25	26	27	28	29	30

MAY / JUNE

MONDAY 28	TUESDAY 29	WEDNESDAY 30	THURSDAY 31
Memorial Day **American Film Festival, New York** (through June 2) "Upstairs, Downstairs" wins Emmy, 1974	Erich Wolfgang Korngold born, 1897 First feature with sound, Griffith's *Dream Street*, opens, 1921	**American Women in Radio and Television Annual Convention, Chicago** (through June 2)	Rainer Werner Fassbinder born, 1946
8:00	8:00	8:00	8:00
9:00	9:00	9:00	9:00
10:00	10:00	10:00	10:00
11:00	11:00	11:00	11:00
Noon	Noon	Noon	Noon
1:00	1:00	1:00	1:00
2:00	2:00	2:00	2:00
3:00	3:00	3:00	3:00
4:00	4:00	4:00	4:00
5:00	5:00	5:00	5:00
6:00	6:00	6:00	6:00
7:00	7:00	7:00	7:00

FRIDAY	SATURDAY
1	*2*
Marilyn Monroe born, 1926	Johnny Weissmuller born, 1904

8:00	
9:00	
10:00	
11:00	
Noon	
1:00	**SUNDAY**
	3
2:00	**National Cable Television Association Annual Convention, Las Vegas** (through June 6)
3:00	Paulette Goddard born, 1911
4:00	
5:00	
6:00	
7:00	

Paulette Goddard born, June 3, 1911 (*The Great Dictator*, with Charlie Chaplin)

APRIL
S	M	T	W	T	F	S
1	2	3	4	5	6	7
8	9	10	11	12	13	14
15	16	17	18	19	20	21
22	23	24	25	26	27	28
29	30					

MAY
S	M	T	W	T	F	S
		1	2	3	4	5
6	7	8	9	10	11	12
13	14	15	16	17	18	19
20	21	22	23	24	25	26
27	28	29	30	31		

JUNE
S	M	T	W	T	F	S
					1	2
3	4	5	6	7	8	9
10	11	12	13	14	15	16
17	18	19	20	21	22	23
24	25	26	27	28	29	30

JUNE

S	M	T	W	T	F	S
					1	2
3	4	5	6	7	8	9
10	11	12	13	14	15	16
17	18	19	20	21	22	23
24	25	26	27	28	29	30

Judy Holliday born, June 21, 1922 (*Born Yesterday*, with William Holden)

JUNE

MONDAY 4	TUESDAY 5	WEDNESDAY 6	THURSDAY 7
Bruce Dern born, 1936	The American Film Institute founded, 1967	First drive-in theater opens, Camden, New Jersey, 1933	First telecast of "The $64,000 Question," 1955
8:00	8:00	8:00	8:00
9:00	9:00	9:00	9:00
10:00	10:00	10:00	10:00
11:00	11:00	11:00	11:00
Noon	Noon	Noon	Noon
1:00	1:00	1:00	1:00
2:00	2:00	2:00	2:00
3:00	3:00	3:00	3:00
4:00	4:00	4:00	4:00
5:00	5:00	5:00	5:00
6:00	6:00	6:00	6:00
7:00	7:00	7:00	7:00

FRIDAY
8

Carl Laemmle founds Universal Film
Manufacturing Co., 1912

Robert Preston born, 1918

8:00

9:00

10:00

11:00

Noon

1:00

2:00

3:00

4:00

5:00

6:00

7:00

SATURDAY
9

Robert Cummings born, 1908

SUNDAY
10

First presentation of 3-D film before
paying audience, Astor Theatre,
New York, 1915

Robert Preston born, June 8, 1918 (*All the Way Home*, with Michael
Kearney)

JUNE

MONDAY *11*	TUESDAY *12*	WEDNESDAY *13*	THURSDAY *14*
Gene Wilder born, 1935 John Wayne dies, 1979	Samuel Z. Arkoff born, 1918 Norma Shearer dies, 1983	**Clio Awards** *Becky Sharp*, first feature in 3-strip Technicolor, opens, 1935	**Flag Day**
8:00	8:00	8:00	8:00
9:00	9:00	9:00	9:00
10:00	10:00	10:00	10:00
11:00	11:00	11:00	11:00
Noon	Noon	Noon	Noon
1:00	1:00	1:00	1:00
2:00	2:00	2:00	2:00
3:00	3:00	3:00	3:00
4:00	4:00	4:00	4:00
5:00	5:00	5:00	5:00
6:00	6:00	6:00	6:00
7:00	7:00	7:00	7:00

FRIDAY
15

Harry Langdon born, 1884

| 8:00 |
| 9:00 |
| 10:00 |
| 11:00 |
| Noon |
| 1:00 |
| 2:00 |
| 3:00 |
| 4:00 |
| 5:00 |
| 6:00 |
| 7:00 |

SATURDAY
16

Psycho opens, 1960

SUNDAY
17

Father's Day

First war footage, of
Spanish-American War, filmed by
Vitagraph, 1898

Gene Wilder born, June 11, 1935 (*Everything You Always Wanted to Know About Sex*)

MAY

S	M	T	W	T	F	S
		1	2	3	4	5
6	7	8	9	10	11	12
13	14	15	16	17	18	19
20	21	22	23	24	25	26
27	28	29	30	31		

JUNE

S	M	T	W	T	F	S
					1	2
3	4	5	6	7	8	9
10	11	12	13	14	15	16
17	18	19	20	21	22	23
24	25	26	27	28	29	30

JULY

S	M	T	W	T	F	S
1	2	3	4	5	6	7
8	9	10	11	12	13	14
15	16	17	18	19	20	21
22	23	24	25	26	27	28
29	30	31				

JUNE

MONDAY *18*	TUESDAY *19*	WEDNESDAY *20*	THURSDAY *21*
Jeanette MacDonald born, 1901 E.G. Marshall born, 1910	First nickelodeon opens, in Pittsburgh, 1905 Gena Rowlands born, 1936	Errol Flynn born, 1909 *Jaws* opens, 1975	Judy Holliday born, 1922
8:00	8:00	8:00	8:00
9:00	9:00	9:00	9:00
10:00	10:00	10:00	10:00
11:00	11:00	11:00	11:00
Noon	Noon	Noon	Noon
1:00	1:00	1:00	1:00
2:00	2:00	2:00	2:00
3:00	3:00	3:00	3:00
4:00	4:00	4:00	4:00
5:00	5:00	5:00	5:00
6:00	6:00	6:00	6:00
7:00	7:00	7:00	7:00

FRIDAY **22**	SATURDAY **23**
Mike Todd born, 1907 *Wild Strawberries* opens in New York, 1959	Bob Fosse born, 1927
8:00	
9:00	
10:00	
11:00	
Noon	
1:00	SUNDAY **24**
2:00	
3:00	Henry King born, 1888 First television use of coaxial cable, Republican National Convention, 1948
4:00	
5:00	
6:00	
7:00	

Bob Fosse born, June 23, 1927 (*Sweet Charity*, with Shirley MacLaine)

MAY							JUNE							JULY						
S	M	T	W	T	F	S	S	M	T	W	T	F	S	S	M	T	W	T	F	S
		1	2	3	4	5						1	2	1	2	3	4	5	6	7
6	7	8	9	10	11	12	3	4	5	6	7	8	9	8	9	10	11	12	13	14
13	14	15	16	17	18	19	10	11	12	13	14	15	16	15	16	17	18	19	20	21
20	21	22	23	24	25	26	17	18	19	20	21	22	23	22	23	24	25	26	27	28
27	28	29	30	31			24	25	26	27	28	29	30	29	30	31				

JUNE/JULY

MONDAY 25	TUESDAY 26	WEDNESDAY 27	THURSDAY 28
Sidney Lumet born, 1924 First commercial color television broadcast, 1951	First movie theater in U.S. opens, New Orleans, 1896 Peter Lorre born, 1904	Bob Keeshan born, 1927	*The King and I* opens, 1956
8:00	8:00	8:00	8:00
9:00	9:00	9:00	9:00
10:00	10:00	10:00	10:00
11:00	11:00	11:00	11:00
Noon	Noon	Noon	Noon
1:00	1:00	1:00	1:00
2:00	2:00	2:00	2:00
3:00	3:00	3:00	3:00
4:00	4:00	4:00	4:00
5:00	5:00	5:00	5:00
6:00	6:00	6:00	6:00
7:00	7:00	7:00	7:00

FRIDAY	SATURDAY
29	**30**
Bernard Herrmann born, 1911	
Slim Pickens born, 1919	
The Thin Man opens, 1934	Susan Hayward born, 1918

8:00	
9:00	
10:00	
11:00	
Noon	
1:00	**SUNDAY**
	1
2:00	
3:00	Charles Laughton born, 1899
	Sydney Pollack born, 1934
4:00	
5:00	
6:00	
7:00	

Sydney Pollack born, July 1, 1934 (*Tootsie*, with Dorothy Michaels)

MAY							JUNE							JULY						
S	M	T	W	T	F	S	S	M	T	W	T	F	S	S	M	T	W	T	F	S
		1	2	3	4	5						1	2	1	2	3	4	5	6	7
6	7	8	9	10	11	12	3	4	5	6	7	8	9	8	9	10	11	12	13	14
13	14	15	16	17	18	19	10	11	12	13	14	15	16	15	16	17	18	19	20	21
20	21	22	23	24	25	26	17	18	19	20	21	22	23	22	23	24	25	26	27	28
27	28	29	30	31			24	25	26	27	28	29	30	29	30	31				

JULY

S	M	T	W	T	F	S
1	2	3	4	5	6	7
8	9	10	11	12	13	14
15	16	17	18	19	20	21
22	23	24	25	26	27	28
29	30	31				

Donald Sutherland born, July 17, 1934 (*M*A*S*H*, with Elliott Gould)

JULY

MONDAY 2	TUESDAY 3	WEDNESDAY 4	THURSDAY 5
			Los Angeles International Film Exposition (through July 20)
Anatomy of a Murder opens, 1959	Ken Russell born, 1927	**Independence Day** Eva Marie Saint born, 1924	Warren Oates born, 1928
8:00	8:00	8:00	8:00
9:00	9:00	9:00	9:00
10:00	10:00	10:00	10:00
11:00	11:00	11:00	11:00
Noon	Noon	Noon	Noon
1:00	1:00	1:00	1:00
2:00	2:00	2:00	2:00
3:00	3:00	3:00	3:00
4:00	4:00	4:00	4:00
5:00	5:00	5:00	5:00
6:00	6:00	6:00	6:00
7:00	7:00	7:00	7:00

FRIDAY 6	SATURDAY 7
First all-talking film, *Lights of New York*, opens, 1928	Vittorio de Sica born, 1902
8:00	
9:00	
10:00	
11:00	
Noon	
1:00	SUNDAY 8
2:00	
3:00	First television series produced in color, "The Marriage," premieres, 1954
4:00	
5:00	
6:00	
7:00	

Eva Marie Saint born, July 4, 1924 (*North by Northwest*, with Cary Grant)

JUNE

S	M	T	W	T	F	S
					1	2
3	4	5	6	7	8	9
10	11	12	13	14	15	16
17	18	19	20	21	22	23
24	25	26	27	28	29	30

JULY

S	M	T	W	T	F	S
1	2	3	4	5	6	7
8	9	10	11	12	13	14
15	16	17	18	19	20	21
22	23	24	25	26	27	28
29	30	31				

AUGUST

S	M	T	W	T	F	S
				1	2	3	4
5	6	7	8	9	10	11
12	13	14	15	16	17	18
19	20	21	22	23	24	25
26	27	28	29	30	31	

JULY

MONDAY 9	TUESDAY 10	WEDNESDAY 11	THURSDAY 12
		First transatlantic transmission by satellite, 1962	George Eastman born, 1854
	John Gilbert born, 1895		Jean Hersholt born, 1886
8:00	8:00	8:00	8:00
9:00	9:00	9:00	9:00
10:00	10:00	10:00	10:00
11:00	11:00	11:00	11:00
Noon	Noon	Noon	Noon
1:00	1:00	1:00	1:00
2:00	2:00	2:00	2:00
3:00	3:00	3:00	3:00
4:00	4:00	4:00	4:00
5:00	5:00	5:00	5:00
6:00	6:00	6:00	6:00
7:00	7:00	7:00	7:00

FRIDAY
13

Harrison Ford born, 1942

SATURDAY
14

Ingmar Bergman born, 1918
Easy Rider opens, 1969

8:00

9:00

10:00

11:00

Noon

1:00

SUNDAY
15

2:00

3:00

4:00

5:00

6:00

7:00

Easy Rider opens, July 14, 1969 (Dennis Hopper, Peter Fonda)

JUNE						
S	M	T	W	T	F	S
					1	2
3	4	5	6	7	8	9
10	11	12	13	14	15	16
17	18	19	20	21	22	23
24	25	26	27	28	29	30

JULY						
S	M	T	W	T	F	S
1	2	3	4	5	6	7
8	9	10	11	12	13	14
15	16	17	18	19	20	21
22	23	24	25	26	27	28
29	30	31				

AUGUST						
S	M	T	W	T	F	S
			1	2	3	4
5	6	7	8	9	10	11
12	13	14	15	16	17	18
19	20	21	22	23	24	25
26	27	28	29	30	31	

JULY

MONDAY 16	TUESDAY 17	WEDNESDAY 18	THURSDAY 19
Barbara Stanwyck born, 1907	Max Fleischer born, 1889 Donald Sutherland born, 1934	Richard Dix born, 1894	Famous Players-Lasky, forerunner of Paramount, incorporated, 1916 TWA introduces first in-flight movie, 1961
8:00	8:00	8:00	8:00
9:00	9:00	9:00	9:00
10:00	10:00	10:00	10:00
11:00	11:00	11:00	11:00
Noon	Noon	Noon	Noon
1:00	1:00	1:00	1:00
2:00	2:00	2:00	2:00
3:00	3:00	3:00	3:00
4:00	4:00	4:00	4:00
5:00	5:00	5:00	5:00
6:00	6:00	6:00	6:00
7:00	7:00	7:00	7:00

FRIDAY
20

Triangle Film corp. formed by D.W. Griffith, Thomas Ince, and Mack Sennett, 1915

8:00	
9:00	
10:00	
11:00	
Noon	
1:00	
2:00	
3:00	
4:00	
5:00	
6:00	
7:00	

SATURDAY
21

CBS begins first regularly scheduled television broadcasting, 1931

SUNDAY
22

James Whale born, 1896

Hercules opens, 1959

James Whale born, July 22, 1896 (*Bride of Frankenstein*, with Colin Clive, Elsa Lanchester, Boris Karloff, Ernest Thesiger)

JUNE

S	M	T	W	T	F	S
					1	2
3	4	5	6	7	8	9
10	11	12	13	14	15	16
17	18	19	20	21	22	23
24	25	26	27	28	29	30

JULY

S	M	T	W	T	F	S
1	2	3	4	5	6	7
8	9	10	11	12	13	14
15	16	17	18	19	20	21
22	23	24	25	26	27	28
29	30	31				

AUGUST

S	M	T	W	T	F	S
				1	2	3	4
5	6	7	8	9	10	11
12	13	14	15	16	17	18
19	20	21	22	23	24	25
26	27	28	29	30	31	

JULY

MONDAY 23	TUESDAY 24	WEDNESDAY 25	THURSDAY 26
			First episode of first film serial, *What Ever Happened to Mary*, released, 1912
Emil Jannings born, 1884	*High Noon* opens, 1952	Walter Brennan born, 1894	
8:00	8:00	8:00	8:00
9:00	9:00	9:00	9:00
10:00	10:00	10:00	10:00
11:00	11:00	11:00	11:00
Noon	Noon	Noon	Noon
1:00	1:00	1:00	1:00
2:00	2:00	2:00	2:00
3:00	3:00	3:00	3:00
4:00	4:00	4:00	4:00
5:00	5:00	5:00	5:00
6:00	6:00	6:00	6:00
7:00	7:00	7:00	7:00

FRIDAY	SATURDAY
27	**28**
Norman Lear born, 1922	*On the Waterfront* opens, 1954
8:00	
9:00	
10:00	
11:00	
Noon	
1:00	SUNDAY
2:00	**29**
3:00	Josef von Sternberg born, 1894
	Clara Bow born, 1904
4:00	
5:00	
6:00	
7:00	

Clara Bow born, July 29, 1904

JUNE

S	M	T	W	T	F	S
					1	2
3	4	5	6	7	8	9
10	11	12	13	14	15	16
17	18	19	20	21	22	23
24	25	26	27	28	29	30

JULY

S	M	T	W	T	F	S
1	2	3	4	5	6	7
8	9	10	11	12	13	14
15	16	17	18	19	20	21
22	23	24	25	26	27	28
29	30	31				

AUGUST

S	M	T	W	T	F	S
			1	2	3	4
5	6	7	8	9	10	11
12	13	14	15	16	17	18
19	20	21	22	23	24	25
26	27	28	29	30	31	

JULY / AUGUST

MONDAY *30*	TUESDAY *31*	WEDNESDAY *1*	THURSDAY *2*
			Jack L. Warner born, 1892 Myrna Loy born, 1905
William Powell born, 1892	Henri Decaë born, 1915		
8:00	8:00	8:00	8:00
9:00	9:00	9:00	9:00
10:00	10:00	10:00	10:00
11:00	11:00	11:00	11:00
Noon	Noon	Noon	Noon
1:00	1:00	1:00	1:00
2:00	2:00	2:00	2:00
3:00	3:00	3:00	3:00
4:00	4:00	4:00	4:00
5:00	5:00	5:00	5:00
6:00	6:00	6:00	6:00
7:00	7:00	7:00	7:00

FRIDAY	SATURDAY
3	*4*

Martin Sheen born, 1940   *Rear Window* opens, 1954

8:00

9:00

10:00

11:00

Noon

SUNDAY

5

1:00

2:00

3:00

John Huston born, 1906

4:00

5:00

6:00

7:00

Rear Window opens, August 4, 1954 (Raymond Burr, James Stewart)

JUNE
S	M	T	W	T	F	S
					1	2
3	4	5	6	7	8	9
10	11	12	13	14	15	16
17	18	19	20	21	22	23
24	25	26	27	28	29	30

JULY
S	M	T	W	T	F	S
1	2	3	4	5	6	7
8	9	10	11	12	13	14
15	16	17	18	19	20	21
22	23	24	25	26	27	28
29	30	31				

AUGUST
S	M	T	W	T	F	S
			1	2	3	4
5	6	7	8	9	10	11
12	13	14	15	16	17	18
19	20	21	22	23	24	25
26	27	28	29	30	31	

AUGUST

S	M	T	W	T	F	S
			1	2	3	4
5	6	7	8	9	10	11
12	13	14	15	16	17	18
19	20	21	22	23	24	25
26	27	28	29	30	31	

Ingrid Bergman born, August 29, 1915 (*Gaslight*)

AUGUST

MONDAY 6	TUESDAY 7	WEDNESDAY 8	THURSDAY 9
First film festival held, as part of Venice Biennale, 1932 *North by Northwest* opens, 1959	Nicholas Ray born, 1911 *The Great Escape* opens, 1963	Sylvia Sidney born, 1910 Esther Williams born, 1923	
8:00	8:00	8:00	8:00
9:00	9:00	9:00	9:00
10:00	10:00	10:00	10:00
11:00	11:00	11:00	11:00
Noon	Noon	Noon	Noon
1:00	1:00	1:00	1:00
2:00	2:00	2:00	2:00
3:00	3:00	3:00	3:00
4:00	4:00	4:00	4:00
5:00	5:00	5:00	5:00
6:00	6:00	6:00	6:00
7:00	7:00	7:00	7:00

FRIDAY *10*	SATURDAY *11*
First telecast of "Candid Camera," 1948	First telecast of ABC News, 1948 *A Hard Day's Night* opens, 1964
8:00	
9:00	
10:00	
11:00	
Noon	
1:00	SUNDAY *12*
2:00	
3:00	Michael Kidd born, 1919
4:00	
5:00	
6:00	
7:00	

Nicholas Ray born, August 7, 1911 (*They Live By Night*, with Cathy O'Donnell, Farley Granger)

JULY

S	M	T	W	T	F	S
1	2	3	4	5	6	7
8	9	10	11	12	13	14
15	16	17	18	19	20	21
22	23	24	25	26	27	28
29	30	31				

AUGUST

S	M	T	W	T	F	S
			1	2	3	4
5	6	7	8	9	10	11
12	13	14	15	16	17	18
19	20	21	22	23	24	25
26	27	28	29	30	31	

SEPTEMBER

S	M	T	W	T	F	S
						1
2	3	4	5	6	7	8
9	10	11	12	13	14	15
16	17	18	19	20	21	22
23	24	25	26	27	28	29
30						

AUGUST

MONDAY 13	TUESDAY 14	WEDNESDAY 15	THURSDAY 16
		Robert Bolt born, 1924 National Television Committee organizes to establish standards for television, 1940	
Alfred Hitchcock born, 1899 *Bonnie and Clyde* opens, 1967			*Cleopatra* opens, 1934
8:00	8:00	8:00	8:00
9:00	9:00	9:00	9:00
10:00	10:00	10:00	10:00
11:00	11:00	11:00	11:00
Noon	Noon	Noon	Noon
1:00	1:00	1:00	1:00
2:00	2:00	2:00	2:00
3:00	3:00	3:00	3:00
4:00	4:00	4:00	4:00
5:00	5:00	5:00	5:00
6:00	6:00	6:00	6:00
7:00	7:00	7:00	7:00

The Wizard of Oz opens, 1939
Robert De Niro born, 1943

8:00

9:00

10:00

11:00

Noon

1:00

2:00

3:00

4:00

5:00

6:00

7:00

Marcel Carne born, 1909
Robert Redford born, 1937

Edinburgh Film and Television Festival (through September 8)

Cleopatra opens, August 16, 1934 (Henry Wilcoxon, Claudette Colbert)

JULY

S	M	T	W	T	F	S
1	2	3	4	5	6	7
8	9	10	11	12	13	14
15	16	17	18	19	20	21
22	23	24	25	26	27	28
29	30	31				

AUGUST

S	M	T	W	T	F	S
				1	2	3	4
5	6	7	8	9	10	11
12	13	14	15	16	17	18
19	20	21	22	23	24	25
26	27	28	29	30	31	

SEPTEMBER

S	M	T	W	T	F	S
						1
2	3	4	5	6	7	8
9	10	11	12	13	14	15
16	17	18	19	20	21	22
23	24	25	26	27	28	29
30						

AUGUST

MONDAY *20*	TUESDAY *21*	WEDNESDAY *22*	THURSDAY *23*
			NBC broadcasts first television series, "The Lost Jungle," 1939 Gene Kelly born, 1912
		Leni Riefenstahl born, 1902	
8:00	8:00	8:00	8:00
9:00	9:00	9:00	9:00
10:00	10:00	10:00	10:00
11:00	11:00	11:00	11:00
Noon	Noon	Noon	Noon
1:00	1:00	1:00	1:00
2:00	2:00	2:00	2:00
3:00	3:00	3:00	3:00
4:00	4:00	4:00	4:00
5:00	5:00	5:00	5:00
6:00	6:00	6:00	6:00
7:00	7:00	7:00	7:00

FRIDAY	SATURDAY
24	*25*
	Ruby Keeler born, 1909
	Sean Connery born, 1930
8:00	
9:00	
10:00	
11:00	
Noon	
1:00	SUNDAY
	26
2:00	
3:00	
4:00	
5:00	
6:00	
7:00	

Sean Connery born, August 25, 1930 (*The Man Who Would Be King*, with Michael Caine)

JULY

S	M	T	W	T	F	S
1	2	3	4	5	6	7
8	9	10	11	12	13	14
15	16	17	18	19	20	21
22	23	24	25	26	27	28
29	30	31				

AUGUST

S	M	T	W	T	F	S
			1	2	3	4
5	6	7	8	9	10	11
12	13	14	15	16	17	18
19	20	21	22	23	24	25
26	27	28	29	30	31	

SEPTEMBER

S	M	T	W	T	F	S
						1
2	3	4	5	6	7	8
9	10	11	12	13	14	15
16	17	18	19	20	21	22
23	24	25	26	27	28	29
30						

AUGUST / SEPTEMBER

MONDAY 27	TUESDAY 28	WEDNESDAY 29	THURSDAY 30
Samuel Goldwyn born, 1882 G.W. Pabst born, 1885 CBS demonstrates color television system, 1940	James Wong Howe born, 1899 Ben Gazzara born, 1930	Ingrid Bergman born, 1915 William Friedkin born, 1939	Donald O'Connor born, 1925 First experimental television broadcast in compatible color, "Kukla, Fran and Ollie," 1953
8:00	8:00	8:00	8:00
9:00	9:00	9:00	9:00
10:00	10:00	10:00	10:00
11:00	11:00	11:00	11:00
Noon	Noon	Noon	Noon
1:00	1:00	1:00	1:00
2:00	2:00	2:00	2:00
3:00	3:00	3:00	3:00
4:00	4:00	4:00	4:00
5:00	5:00	5:00	5:00
6:00	6:00	6:00	6:00
7:00	7:00	7:00	7:00

FRIDAY
31

Telluride Film Festival (through September 3)
Dore Schary born, 1905

8:00

9:00

10:00

11:00

Noon

1:00

2:00

3:00

4:00

5:00

6:00

7:00

SATURDAY
1

First film school, State School of Cinematography, founded, Moscow, 1919

SUNDAY
2

Donald O'Connor born, August 30, 1925 (*The Milkman*)

JULY

S	M	T	W	T	F	S
1	2	3	4	5	6	7
8	9	10	11	12	13	14
15	16	17	18	19	20	21
22	23	24	25	26	27	28
29	30	31				

AUGUST

S	M	T	W	T	F	S
			1	2	3	4
5	6	7	8	9	10	11
12	13	14	15	16	17	18
19	20	21	22	23	24	25
26	27	28	29	30	31	

SEPTEMBER

S	M	T	W	T	F	S
						1
2	3	4	5	6	7	8
9	10	11	12	13	14	15
16	17	18	19	20	21	22
23	24	25	26	27	28	29
30						

SEPTEMBER

S	M	T	W	T	F	S
						1
2	3	4	5	6	7	8
9	10	11	12	13	14	15
16	17	18	19	20	21	22
23	24	25	26	27	28	29
30	31					

Mickey Rooney born, September 23, 1920

ORDER FORM
1985
AFI Desk Diary

INDIVIDUAL DIARY ORDER

Please send me the following copies of the 1985 AFI Desk Diary:

Quantity   **Total Amount**

_____ copies @ the AFI Member
Price of $16.00 $ _____

_____ copies @ the Non-
Member Price of $17.95 $ _____

_____ **PLUS** shipping and
handling charges $ _____ **··**

_____ copies sent outside U.S.A.
and Canada, add interna-
tional postage and handling
@ $5.50 for each copy $ _____

_____ **TOTAL**   **TOTAL**
COPIES   **AMOUNT DUE:** $ _____

**1985 Desk Diary Shipping Information

Order Value	Shipping/Handling Charge
$1-$20.00	$3.00
$21-$50.00	$5.00
$51-$100.00	$8.50
$101 and above	$11.00

☐ My check/money order is enclosed payable in U.S.
dollars to The American Film Institute in the
amount of $ _____

_____
Name

_____
Address

_____
City

_____
State   Zip

_____
Telephone (Daytime)   DD84

Bulk Order

The 1985 AFI Desk Diary will make a handsome gift for friends, clients, and associates. Following is a bulk price list that enables you to *save* when you order in quantities of ten or more.

Quantity	Price
10-25	$14.00 each
26-50	$13.00 each
51-100	$12.00 each
101-250	$11.00 each
251-499	$10.00 each
500 or more	$ 8.50 each

**Please add $1.00 per diary for shipping and han-
dling of bulk orders.**

☐ Please send _____ copies of the 1985 AFI
Desk Diary at the special bulk (10 or more) rate of
$ _____ described above.

☐ My check/money order is enclosed payable in U.S.
dollars to The American Film Institute in the
amount of $ _____ .

Mail To:
AFI Desk Diary
The American Film Institute
5104 MacArthur Boulevard, NW
Washington, D.C. 20016

For Additional Information, call
202/364-8006.

TURN OVER FOR ADDITIONAL GIFT ORDER FORM.

Last chance
to order next year's
AFI DESK DIARY
at last year's prices.

Now is the time to reserve your copies of the 1985 AFI Desk Diary. Next year's edition will exhibit the same careful editing and tasteful design. You'll find new and updated information and more memorable photographs from film and television of the past. The AFI Desk Diary is a gift item you can give with confidence to your choosiest friends, clients and associates. Place your order today!

SEPTEMBER

MONDAY 3	TUESDAY 4	WEDNESDAY 5	THURSDAY 6
Labor Day First television soap opera, "Search for Tomorrow," premieres, 1951	Sweden establishes first state censorship board, 1911	Darryl F. Zannuck born, 1902 Jack Valenti born, 1921	*The Phantom of the Opera* opens, 1925 *Top Hat* opens, 1935
8:00	8:00	8:00	8:00
9:00	9:00	9:00	9:00
10:00	10:00	10:00	10:00
11:00	11:00	11:00	11:00
Noon	Noon	Noon	Noon
1:00	1:00	1:00	1:00
2:00	2:00	2:00	2:00
3:00	3:00	3:00	3:00
4:00	4:00	4:00	4:00
5:00	5:00	5:00	5:00
6:00	6:00	6:00	6:00
7:00	7:00	7:00	7:00

FRIDAY 7	SATURDAY 8
Elia Kazan born, 1909	"Star Trek" premieres, 1966
8:00	
9:00	
10:00	
11:00	
Noon	
1:00	**SUNDAY** **9**
2:00	
3:00	"Roots" receives Emmy for Best Limited Series, 1979
4:00	
5:00	
6:00	
7:00	

"Roots" receives Emmy for Best Limited Series, September 9, 1979
(Madge Sinclair, John Amos)

AUGUST

S	M	T	W	T	F	S
			1	2	3	4
5	6	7	8	9	10	11
12	13	14	15	16	17	18
19	20	21	22	23	24	25
26	27	28	29	30	31	

SEPTEMBER

S	M	T	W	T	F	S
						1
2	3	4	5	6	7	8
9	10	11	12	13	14	15
16	17	18	19	20	21	22
23	24	25	26	27	28	29
30						

OCTOBER

S	M	T	W	T	F	S
	1	2	3	4	5	6
7	8	9	10	11	12	13
14	15	16	17	18	19	20
21	22	23	24	25	26	27
28	29	30	31			

SEPTEMBER

MONDAY 10	TUESDAY 11	WEDNESDAY 12	THURSDAY 13
Robert Wise born, 1914 "Gunsmoke" premieres, 1955	"Little House on the Prairie" premieres, 1974	"Bonanza" premieres, 1959	"The Rockford Files" premieres, 1974
8:00	8:00	8:00	8:00
9:00	9:00	9:00	9:00
10:00	10:00	10:00	10:00
11:00	11:00	11:00	11:00
Noon	Noon	Noon	Noon
1:00	1:00	1:00	1:00
2:00	2:00	2:00	2:00
3:00	3:00	3:00	3:00
4:00	4:00	4:00	4:00
5:00	5:00	5:00	5:00
6:00	6:00	6:00	6:00
7:00	7:00	7:00	7:00

FRIDAY	SATURDAY
14	*15*
	Jean Renoir born, 1894
8:00	
9:00	
10:00	
11:00	
Noon	
1:00	SUNDAY
2:00	*16*
3:00	Alexander Korda born, 1893 Peter Falk born, 1927
4:00	
5:00	
6:00	
7:00	

"The Rockford Files" premieres, September 13, 1974 (Noah Beery, Jr., James Garner)

AUGUST

S	M	T	W	T	F	S
				1	2	3	4
5	6	7	8	9	10	11
12	13	14	15	16	17	18
19	20	21	22	23	24	25
26	27	28	29	30	31	

SEPTEMBER

S	M	T	W	T	F	S
						1
2	3	4	5	6	7	8
9	10	11	12	13	14	15
16	17	18	19	20	21	22
23	24	25	26	27	28	29
30						

OCTOBER

S	M	T	W	T	F	S
	1	2	3	4	5	6
7	8	9	10	11	12	13
14	15	16	17	18	19	20
21	22	23	24	25	26	27
28	29	30	31			

SEPTEMBER

MONDAY 17	TUESDAY 18	WEDNESDAY 19	THURSDAY 20
			First Cannes Film Festival opens, 1946 "The Jackie Gleason Show" premieres, 1952
Roddy McDowall born, 1928 Anne Bancroft born, 1931	Greta Garbo born, 1905	Frances Farmer born, 1913	
8:00	8:00	8:00	8:00
9:00	9:00	9:00	9:00
10:00	10:00	10:00	10:00
11:00	11:00	11:00	11:00
Noon	Noon	Noon	Noon
1:00	1:00	1:00	1:00
2:00	2:00	2:00	2:00
3:00	3:00	3:00	3:00
4:00	4:00	4:00	4:00
5:00	5:00	5:00	5:00
6:00	6:00	6:00	6:00
7:00	7:00	7:00	7:00

FRIDAY	SATURDAY
21	*22*

First Technicolor film, *The Gulf Between Us*, opens, 1917

Erich von Stroheim born, 1885
Paul Muni born, 1895
Sabrina opens, 1954

8:00

9:00

10:00

11:00

Noon

1:00

SUNDAY

23

2:00

3:00

Mickey Rooney born, 1920
Romy Schneider born, 1938

4:00

5:00

6:00

7:00

Frances Farmer born, September 19, 1913 (*Flowing Gold*, with John Garfield and Pat O'Brien)

AUGUST
S	M	T	W	T	F	S
			1	2	3	4
5	6	7	8	9	10	11
12	13	14	15	16	17	18
19	20	21	22	23	24	25
26	27	28	29	30	31	

SEPTEMBER
S	M	T	W	T	F	S
						1
2	3	4	5	6	7	8
9	10	11	12	13	14	15
16	17	18	19	20	21	22
23	24	25	26	27	28	29
30						

OCTOBER
S	M	T	W	T	F	S
	1	2	3	4	5	6
7	8	9	10	11	12	13
14	15	16	17	18	19	20
21	22	23	24	25	26	27
28	29	30	31			

SEPTEMBER

MONDAY 24	TUESDAY 25	WEDNESDAY 26	THURSDAY 27
Mary Poppins opens, 1964 First telecast of "60 Minutes," 1968		William Paley becomes president of CBS, 1928 *The Three Faces of Eve* opens, 1957	**Rosh Hashanah** "The Tonight Show" premieres, 1954 "Caesar's Hour" premieres, 1954
8:00	8:00	8:00	8:00
9:00	9:00	9:00	9:00
10:00	10:00	10:00	10:00
11:00	11:00	11:00	11:00
Noon	Noon	Noon	Noon
1:00	1:00	1:00	1:00
2:00	2:00	2:00	2:00
3:00	3:00	3:00	3:00
4:00	4:00	4:00	4:00
5:00	5:00	5:00	5:00
6:00	6:00	6:00	6:00
7:00	7:00	7:00	7:00

FRIDAY	SATURDAY
28	*29*
John Sayles born, 1950	Gene Autry born, 1907

8:00	
9:00	
10:00	
11:00	
Noon	

1:00	SUNDAY
	30
2:00	
3:00	World Series telecast for first time, 1947
	"The Red Skelton Show" premieres, 1951
4:00	
5:00	
6:00	
7:00	

"The Red Skelton Show" premieres, September 30, 1951

AUGUST							SEPTEMBER							OCTOBER						
S	M	T	W	T	F	S	S	M	T	W	T	F	S	S	M	T	W	T	F	S
			1	2	3	4							1		1	2	3	4	5	6
5	6	7	8	9	10	11	2	3	4	5	6	7	8	7	8	9	10	11	12	13
12	13	14	15	16	17	18	9	10	11	12	13	14	15	14	15	16	17	18	19	20
19	20	21	22	23	24	25	16	17	18	19	20	21	22	21	22	23	24	25	26	27
26	27	28	29	30	31		23	24	25	26	27	28	29	28	29	30	31			
							30													

October

S	M	T	W	T	F	S
	1	2	3	4	5	6
7	8	9	10	11	12	13
14	15	16	17	18	19	20
21	22	23	24	25	26	27
28	29	30	31			

Rouben Mamoulian born, October 8, 1898 (*Love Me Tonight*, with Jeanette MacDonald, Maurice Chevalier)

OCTOBER

MONDAY	TUESDAY	WEDNESDAY	THURSDAY
1	*2*	*3*	*4*
	Groucho Marx born, 1890		
	"Alfred Hitchcock Presents" premieres, 1955		First telecast of "Playhouse 90," 1956
Walter Matthau born, 1920	"The Twilight Zone" premieres, 1959	*The Maltese Falcon* opens, 1941	"Leave It to Beaver" premieres, 1957
"This Is Your Life" premieres, 1952		"Father Knows Best" premieres, 1954	
8:00	8:00	8:00	8:00
9:00	9:00	9:00	9:00
10:00	10:00	10:00	10:00
11:00	11:00	11:00	11:00
Noon	Noon	Noon	Noon
1:00	1:00	1:00	1:00
2:00	2:00	2:00	2:00
3:00	3:00	3:00	3:00
4:00	4:00	4:00	4:00
5:00	5:00	5:00	5:00
6:00	6:00	6:00	6:00
7:00	7:00	7:00	7:00

FRIDAY
5

Louis Lumiere born, 1864

8:00	
9:00	
10:00	
11:00	
Noon	
1:00	
2:00	
3:00	
4:00	
5:00	
6:00	
7:00	

SATURDAY
6

Yom Kippur
Pillow Talk opens, 1959

SUNDAY
7

"The Twilight Zone" premieres, October 2, 1959 (William Shatner and Pat Breslin in "Nick of Time")

SEPTEMBER						
S	M	T	W	T	F	S
						1
2	3	4	5	6	7	8
9	10	11	12	13	14	15
16	17	18	19	20	21	22
23	24	25	26	27	28	29
30						

OCTOBER						
S	M	T	W	T	F	S
		1	2	3	4	5	6
7	8	9	10	11	12	13
14	15	16	17	18	19	20
21	22	23	24	25	26	27
28	29	30	31			

NOVEMBER						
S	M	T	W	T	F	S
					1	2	3
4	5	6	7	8	9	10
11	12	13	14	15	16	17
18	19	20	21	22	23	24
25	26	27	28	29	30	

OCTOBER

MONDAY *8*	TUESDAY *9*	WEDNESDAY *10*	THURSDAY *11*
Columbus Day Rouben Mamoulian born, 1898	Jacques Tati born, 1908	Harold Pinter born, 1930	*To Have and Have Not* opens, 1944
8:00	8:00	8:00	8:00
9:00	9:00	9:00	9:00
10:00	10:00	10:00	10:00
11:00	11:00	11:00	11:00
Noon	Noon	Noon	Noon
1:00	1:00	1:00	1:00
2:00	2:00	2:00	2:00
3:00	3:00	3:00	3:00
4:00	4:00	4:00	4:00
5:00	5:00	5:00	5:00
6:00	6:00	6:00	6:00
7:00	7:00	7:00	7:00

FRIDAY	SATURDAY
12	*13*
	First television broadcast from the White House, 1947
8:00	
9:00	
10:00	
11:00	
Noon	
1:00	SUNDAY
2:00	*14*
3:00	Lillian Gish born, 1896
4:00	
5:00	
6:00	
7:00	

To Have and Have Not opens, October 11, 1944 (Humphrey Bogart, Lauren Bacall, Dan Seymour)

SEPTEMBER

S	M	T	W	T	F	S
						1
2	3	4	5	6	7	8
9	10	11	12	13	14	15
16	17	18	19	20	21	22
23	24	25	26	27	28	29
30						

OCTOBER

S	M	T	W	T	F	S
	1	2	3	4	5	6
7	8	9	10	11	12	13
14	15	16	17	18	19	20
21	22	23	24	25	26	27
28	29	30	31			

NOVEMBER

S	M	T	W	T	F	S
				1	2	3
4	5	6	7	8	9	10
11	12	13	14	15	16	17
18	19	20	21	22	23	24
25	26	27	28	29	30	

OCTOBER

MONDAY 15	TUESDAY 16	WEDNESDAY 17	THURSDAY 18
"I Love Lucy" premieres, 1951 "The Untouchables" premieres, 1959	Angela Lansbury born, 1925	Jean Arthur born, 1926	Lamar Trotti born, 1900 George C. Scott born, 1927
8:00	8:00	8:00	8:00
9:00	9:00	9:00	9:00
10:00	10:00	10:00	10:00
11:00	11:00	11:00	11:00
Noon	Noon	Noon	Noon
1:00	1:00	1:00	1:00
2:00	2:00	2:00	2:00
3:00	3:00	3:00	3:00
4:00	4:00	4:00	4:00
5:00	5:00	5:00	5:00
6:00	6:00	6:00	6:00
7:00	7:00	7:00	7:00

FRIDAY
19

Paramount stockholders agree to takeover by Gulf + Western, 1966

8:00	
9:00	
10:00	
11:00	
Noon	
1:00	
2:00	
3:00	
4:00	
5:00	
6:00	
7:00	

SATURDAY
20

Bela Lugosi born, 1882

SUNDAY
21

My Fair Lady opens, 1964

First telecast of "Monday Night Football," 1970

"I Love Lucy" premieres, October 15, 1951

SEPTEMBER

S	M	T	W	T	F	S
						1
2	3	4	5	6	7	8
9	10	11	12	13	14	15
16	17	18	19	20	21	22
23	24	25	26	27	28	29
30						

OCTOBER

S	M	T	W	T	F	S
	1	2	3	4	5	6
7	8	9	10	11	12	13
14	15	16	17	18	19	20
21	22	23	24	25	26	27
28	29	30	31			

NOVEMBER

S	M	T	W	T	F	S
					1	2	3
4	5	6	7	8	9	10
11	12	13	14	15	16	17
18	19	20	21	22	23	24
25	26	27	28	29	30	

October

MONDAY 22	TUESDAY 23	WEDNESDAY 24	THURSDAY 25
Joan Fontaine born, 1917	Johnny Carson born, 1925		
8:00	8:00	8:00	8:00
9:00	9:00	9:00	9:00
10:00	10:00	10:00	10:00
11:00	11:00	11:00	11:00
Noon	Noon	Noon	Noon
1:00	1:00	1:00	1:00
2:00	2:00	2:00	2:00
3:00	3:00	3:00	3:00
4:00	4:00	4:00	4:00
5:00	5:00	5:00	5:00
6:00	6:00	6:00	6:00
7:00	7:00	7:00	7:00

FRIDAY
26

Rebel Without a Cause opens, twenty-six days after James Dean's death, 1955

8:00	
9:00	
10:00	
11:00	
Noon	
1:00	
2:00	
3:00	
4:00	
5:00	
6:00	
7:00	

SATURDAY
27

Society of Motion Picture and Television Engineers Convention, New York (through November 3)

SUNDAY
28

First sound newsreel presented, 1928

"The Jack Benny Show" premieres, 1950

Joan Fontaine born, October 22, 1917 (*Suspicion*, with Cary Grant)

SEPTEMBER						
S	M	T	W	T	F	S
						1
2	3	4	5	6	7	8
9	10	11	12	13	14	15
16	17	18	19	20	21	22
23	24	25	26	27	28	29
30						

OCTOBER						
S	M	T	W	T	F	S
	1	2	3	4	5	6
7	8	9	10	11	12	13
14	15	16	17	18	19	20
21	22	23	24	25	26	27
28	29	30	31			

NOVEMBER						
S	M	T	W	T	F	S
					1	2	3
4	5	6	7	8	9	10
11	12	13	14	15	16	17
18	19	20	21	22	23	24
25	26	27	28	29	30	

OCTOBER / NOVEMBER

MONDAY 29	TUESDAY 30	WEDNESDAY 31	THURSDAY 1
		Halloween **International Film & TV Festival of New York** (through November 2)	
	National Association of Theatre Owners Convention, Washington, D.C. (through November 4)		MPAA ratings go into effect, 1968
Akim Tamiroff born, 1899		Ethel Waters born, 1899	King Vidor dies, 1982
8:00	8:00	8:00	8:00
9:00	9:00	9:00	9:00
10:00	10:00	10:00	10:00
11:00	11:00	11:00	11:00
Noon	Noon	Noon	Noon
1:00	1:00	1:00	1:00
2:00	2:00	2:00	2:00
3:00	3:00	3:00	3:00
4:00	4:00	4:00	4:00
5:00	5:00	5:00	5:00
6:00	6:00	6:00	6:00
7:00	7:00	7:00	7:00

FRIDAY
2

Burt Lancaster born, 1913

SATURDAY
3

First transcontinental television transmission in color, 1953

8:00	
9:00	
10:00	
11:00	
Noon	

SUNDAY
4

Chicago International Film Festival (through November 18)

1:00	
2:00	
3:00	
4:00	
5:00	
6:00	
7:00	

Ethel Waters born, October 31, 1899 (*Pinky*, with Jeanne Crain)

NOVEMBER

S	M	T	W	T	F	S
				1	2	3
4	5	6	7	8	9	10
11	12	13	14	15	16	17
18	19	20	21	22	23	24
25	26	27	28	29	30	

Robert Ryan born, November 11, 1908 (*The Wild Bunch*)

November

MONDAY 5	TUESDAY 6	WEDNESDAY 7	THURSDAY 8
Joel McCrea born, 1905 Jacques Tati dies, 1982	*The Sheik* opens, 1921	Herman J. Mankiewicz born, 1897 First telecast of "Face the Nation," 1954	Katharine Hepburn born, 1907 *All the King's Men* opens, 1949
8:00	8:00	8:00	8:00
9:00	9:00	9:00	9:00
10:00	10:00	10:00	10:00
11:00	11:00	11:00	11:00
Noon	Noon	Noon	Noon
1:00	1:00	1:00	1:00
2:00	2:00	2:00	2:00
3:00	3:00	3:00	3:00
4:00	4:00	4:00	4:00
5:00	5:00	5:00	5:00
6:00	6:00	6:00	6:00
7:00	7:00	7:00	7:00

FRIDAY	SATURDAY
9	*10*
Mae Marsh born, 1895	
Hedy Lamarr born, 1913	Claude Rains born, 1889

8:00	
9:00	
10:00	
11:00	
Noon	

1:00	SUNDAY
	11
2:00	
	Veterans Day
3:00	Robert Ryan born, 1909
	Gentleman's Agreement opens, 1947
4:00	
5:00	
6:00	
7:00	

Gentleman's Agreement opens, November 11, 1947 (Dorothy McGuire, Gregory Peck, John Garfield)

OCTOBER						
S	M	T	W	T	F	S
	1	2	3	4	5	6
7	8	9	10	11	12	13
14	15	16	17	18	19	20
21	22	23	24	25	26	27
28	29	30	31			

NOVEMBER						
S	M	T	W	T	F	S
				1	2	3
4	5	6	7	8	9	10
11	12	13	14	15	16	17
18	19	20	21	22	23	24
25	26	27	28	29	30	

DECEMBER						
S	M	T	W	T	F	S
						1
2	3	4	5	6	7	8
9	10	11	12	13	14	15
16	17	18	19	20	21	22
23	24	25	26	27	28	29
30	31					

November

MONDAY 12	TUESDAY 13	WEDNESDAY 14	THURSDAY 15
		Dick Powell born, 1904	
	Henri Langlois born, 1894	Veronica Lake born, 1919	*The Gay Divorcee* opens, 1934
8:00	8:00	8:00	8:00
9:00	9:00	9:00	9:00
10:00	10:00	10:00	10:00
11:00	11:00	11:00	11:00
Noon	Noon	Noon	Noon
1:00	1:00	1:00	1:00
2:00	2:00	2:00	2:00
3:00	3:00	3:00	3:00
4:00	4:00	4:00	4:00
5:00	5:00	5:00	5:00
6:00	6:00	6:00	6:00
7:00	7:00	7:00	7:00

FRIDAY
16

Mabel Normand born, 1894

First cartoon, *The Enchanted Drawing*, copyrighted, 1900

8:00	
9:00	
10:00	
11:00	
Noon	
1:00	
2:00	
3:00	
4:00	
5:00	
6:00	
7:00	

SATURDAY
17

Lee Strasberg born, 1901

Rock Hudson born, 1925

Martin Scorsese born, 1942

SUNDAY
18

Ben-Hur opens, 1959

Lee Strasberg born, November 17, 1901 (*Going in Style*, with George Burns, Art Carney)

OCTOBER						
S	M	T	W	T	F	S
	1	2	3	4	5	6
7	8	9	10	11	12	13
14	15	16	17	18	19	20
21	22	23	24	25	26	27
28	29	30	31			

NOVEMBER						
S	M	T	W	T	F	S
				1	2	3
4	5	6	7	8	9	10
11	12	13	14	15	16	17
18	19	20	21	22	23	24
25	26	27	28	29	30	

DECEMBER						
S	M	T	W	T	F	S
						1
2	3	4	5	6	7	8
9	10	11	12	13	14	15
16	17	18	19	20	21	22
23	24	25	26	27	28	29
30	31					

November

MONDAY 19	TUESDAY 20	WEDNESDAY 21	THURSDAY 22
Dick Cavett born, 1936 Jodie Foster born, 1962	Estelle Parsons born, 1927	*The Best Years of Our Lives* opens, 1946	**Thanksgiving** Geraldine Page born, 1924
8:00	8:00	8:00	8:00
9:00	9:00	9:00	9:00
10:00	10:00	10:00	10:00
11:00	11:00	11:00	11:00
Noon	Noon	Noon	Noon
1:00	1:00	1:00	1:00
2:00	2:00	2:00	2:00
3:00	3:00	3:00	3:00
4:00	4:00	4:00	4:00
5:00	5:00	5:00	5:00
6:00	6:00	6:00	6:00
7:00	7:00	7:00	7:00

FRIDAY
23

Boris Karloff born, 1887
The Magnificent Seven opens,
1960

8:00	
9:00	
10:00	
11:00	
Noon	
1:00	
2:00	
3:00	
4:00	
5:00	
6:00	
7:00	

SATURDAY
24

Garson Kanin born, 1912
Geraldine Fitzgerald born, 1924

SUNDAY
25

W.R. Burnett born, 1899

Jodie Foster born, November 19, 1962 (*Foxes*)

OCTOBER							NOVEMBER							DECEMBER						
S	M	T	W	T	F	S	S	M	T	W	T	F	S	S	M	T	W	T	F	S
	1	2	3	4	5	6					1	2	3							1
7	8	9	10	11	12	13	4	5	6	7	8	9	10	2	3	4	5	6	7	8
14	15	16	17	18	19	20	11	12	13	14	15	16	17	9	10	11	12	13	14	15
21	22	23	24	25	26	27	18	19	20	21	22	23	24	16	17	18	19	20	21	22
28	29	30	31				25	26	27	28	29	30		23	24	25	26	27	28	29
														30	31					

November/December

MONDAY *26*	TUESDAY *27*	WEDNESDAY *28*	THURSDAY *29*
Eric Sevareid born, 1912 *Casablanca* opens, 1942	Bruce Lee born, 1940	Gloria Grahame born, 1924	Busby Berkeley born, 1895 Yakima Canutt born, 1895
8:00	8:00	8:00	8:00
9:00	9:00	9:00	9:00
10:00	10:00	10:00	10:00
11:00	11:00	11:00	11:00
Noon	Noon	Noon	Noon
1:00	1:00	1:00	1:00
2:00	2:00	2:00	2:00
3:00	3:00	3:00	3:00
4:00	4:00	4:00	4:00
5:00	5:00	5:00	5:00
6:00	6:00	6:00	6:00
7:00	7:00	7:00	7:00

FRIDAY
30

8:00	
9:00	
10:00	
11:00	
Noon	
1:00	
2:00	
3:00	
4:00	
5:00	
6:00	
7:00	

SATURDAY
1

Woody Allen born, 1935

Richard Pryor born, 1940

SUNDAY
2

Bruce Lee born, November 27, 1940 (*Enter the Dragon*)

OCTOBER

S	M	T	W	T	F	S
	1	2	3	4	5	6
7	8	9	10	11	12	13
14	15	16	17	18	19	20
21	22	23	24	25	26	27
28	29	30	31			

NOVEMBER

S	M	T	W	T	F	S
				1	2	3
4	5	6	7	8	9	10
11	12	13	14	15	16	17
18	19	20	21	22	23	24
25	26	27	28	29	30	

DECEMBER

S	M	T	W	T	F	S
						1
2	3	4	5	6	7	8
9	10	11	12	13	14	15
16	17	18	19	20	21	22
23	24	25	26	27	28	29
30	31					

DECEMBER

S	M	T	W	T	F	S
						1
2	3	4	5	6	7	8
9	10	11	12	13	14	15
16	17	18	19	20	21	22
23	24	25	26	27	28	29
30	31					

John Cassavetes born, December 9, 1929 (*The Fury*)

December

MONDAY 3	TUESDAY 4	WEDNESDAY 5	THURSDAY 6
Sven Nykvist born, 1922 Jean-Luc Godard born, 1930	*Frankenstein* opens, 1931 Jeff Bridges born, 1949	Otto Preminger born, 1906 Abraham Polonsky born, 1910	William S. Hart born, 1870 *A Night at the Opera* opens, 1935
8:00	8:00	8:00	8:00
9:00	9:00	9:00	9:00
10:00	10:00	10:00	10:00
11:00	11:00	11:00	11:00
Noon	Noon	Noon	Noon
1:00	1:00	1:00	1:00
2:00	2:00	2:00	2:00
3:00	3:00	3:00	3:00
4:00	4:00	4:00	4:00
5:00	5:00	5:00	5:00
6:00	6:00	6:00	6:00
7:00	7:00	7:00	7:00

FRIDAY *7*	SATURDAY *8*
Ellen Burstyn born, 1932	George Méliès born, 1861
8:00	
9:00	
10:00	
11:00	
Noon	
1:00	SUNDAY *9*
2:00	
3:00	Dalton Trumbo born, 1905 John Cassavetes born, 1929
4:00	
5:00	
6:00	
7:00	

Dalton Trumbo born, December 9, 1905 (*Papillon*, with Steve McQueen and Dustin Hoffman)

NOVEMBER						
S	M	T	W	T	F	S
					1	2	3
4	5	6	7	8	9	10
11	12	13	14	15	16	17
18	19	20	21	22	23	24
25	26	27	28	29	30	

DECEMBER						
S	M	T	W	T	F	S
						1
2	3	4	5	6	7	8
9	10	11	12	13	14	15
16	17	18	19	20	21	22
23	24	25	26	27	28	29
30	31					

JANUARY						
S	M	T	W	T	F	S
		1	2	3	4	5
6	7	8	9	10	11	12
13	14	15	16	17	18	19
20	21	22	23	24	25	26
27	28	29	30	31		

DECEMBER

MONDAY 10	TUESDAY 11	WEDNESDAY 12	THURSDAY 13
	Guess Who's Coming to Dinner opens, 1967		
Victor McLaglen born, 1886		Frank Sinatra born, 1915	Christopher Plummer born, 1927
8:00	8:00	8:00	8:00
9:00	9:00	9:00	9:00
10:00	10:00	10:00	10:00
11:00	11:00	11:00	11:00
Noon	Noon	Noon	Noon
1:00	1:00	1:00	1:00
2:00	2:00	2:00	2:00
3:00	3:00	3:00	3:00
4:00	4:00	4:00	4:00
5:00	5:00	5:00	5:00
6:00	6:00	6:00	6:00
7:00	7:00	7:00	7:00

FRIDAY	SATURDAY
14	*15*
Lee Remick born, 1935 Patty Duke born, 1946	*Exodus* opens, 1960
8:00	
9:00	
10:00	
11:00	
Noon	
1:00	SUNDAY
2:00	*16*
3:00	
4:00	Liv Ullmann born, 1939
5:00	
6:00	
7:00	

Frank Sinatra born, December 12, 1915 (*From Here to Eternity*, with Montgomery Clift)

NOVEMBER

S	M	T	W	T	F	S
					1	2	3
4	5	6	7	8	9	10
11	12	13	14	15	16	17
18	19	20	21	22	23	24
25	26	27	28	29	30	

DECEMBER

S	M	T	W	T	F	S
						1
2	3	4	5	6	7	8
9	10	11	12	13	14	15
16	17	18	19	20	21	22
23	24	25	26	27	28	29
30	31					

JANUARY

S	M	T	W	T	F	S
		1	2	3	4	5
6	7	8	9	10	11	12
13	14	15	16	17	18	19
20	21	22	23	24	25	26
27	28	29	30	31		

December

MONDAY 17	TUESDAY 18	WEDNESDAY 19	THURSDAY 20
On the Beach opens, 1959 Atlanta's WTCG (now WTBS) becomes first commercial TV station to distribute via satellite to cable systems, 1976	Betty Grable born, 1916	**First Day of Hanukkah** Cicely Tyson born, 1939	George Roy Hill born, 1922
8:00	8:00	8:00	8:00
9:00	9:00	9:00	9:00
10:00	10:00	10:00	10:00
11:00	11:00	11:00	11:00
Noon	Noon	Noon	Noon
1:00	1:00	1:00	1:00
2:00	2:00	2:00	2:00
3:00	3:00	3:00	3:00
4:00	4:00	4:00	4:00
5:00	5:00	5:00	5:00
6:00	6:00	6:00	6:00
7:00	7:00	7:00	7:00

FRIDAY
21

The Graduate opens, 1967

8:00

9:00

10:00

11:00

Noon

1:00

2:00

3:00

4:00

5:00

6:00

7:00

SATURDAY
22

SUNDAY
23

Cicely Tyson born, December 19, 1939 (*Sounder,* with Kevin Hooks)

NOVEMBER

S	M	T	W	T	F	S
				1	2	3
4	5	6	7	8	9	10
11	12	13	14	15	16	17
18	19	20	21	22	23	24
25	26	27	28	29	30	

DECEMBER

S	M	T	W	T	F	S
						1
2	3	4	5	6	7	8
9	10	11	12	13	14	15
16	17	18	19	20	21	22
23	24	25	26	27	28	29
30	31					

JANUARY

S	M	T	W	T	F	S
		1	2	3	4	5
6	7	8	9	10	11	12
13	14	15	16	17	18	19
20	21	22	23	24	25	26
27	28	29	30	31		

December

MONDAY 24	TUESDAY 25	WEDNESDAY 26	THURSDAY 27
	Christmas		
Ava Gardner born, 1922	Humphrey Bogart born, 1899 Sissy Spacek born, 1949	Richard Widmark born, 1914 Steve Allen born, 1921	Marlene Dietrich born, 1901 Radio City Music Hall opens, 1932
8:00	8:00	8:00	8:00
9:00	9:00	9:00	9:00
10:00	10:00	10:00	10:00
11:00	11:00	11:00	11:00
Noon	Noon	Noon	Noon
1:00	1:00	1:00	1:00
2:00	2:00	2:00	2:00
3:00	3:00	3:00	3:00
4:00	4:00	4:00	4:00
5:00	5:00	5:00	5:00
6:00	6:00	6:00	6:00
7:00	7:00	7:00	7:00

FRIDAY	SATURDAY
28	**29**
F.W. Murnau born, 1888	
Maggie Smith born, 1934	Mary Tyler Moore born, 1937

8:00

9:00

10:00

11:00

Noon

1:00

SUNDAY

30

2:00

3:00

Ben-Hur opens, 1925

4:00

5:00

6:00

7:00

Sissy Spacek born, December 25, 1949 (*Coal Miner's Daughter*, with Levon Helm)

NOVEMBER								DECEMBER								JANUARY						
S	M	T	W	T	F	S		S	M	T	W	T	F	S		S	M	T	W	T	F	S
				1	2	3								1				1	2	3	4	5
4	5	6	7	8	9	10		2	3	4	5	6	7	8		6	7	8	9	10	11	12
11	12	13	14	15	16	17		9	10	11	12	13	14	15		13	14	15	16	17	18	19
18	19	20	21	22	23	24		16	17	18	19	20	21	22		20	21	22	23	24	25	26
25	26	27	28	29	30			23	24	25	26	27	28	29		27	28	29	30	31		
								30	31													

December/January

MONDAY *31*	TUESDAY *1*	WEDNESDAY *2*	THURSDAY *3*
	New Year's Day Patent for iconoscope-kinescope tubes granted to Dr. Vladimir Zworkin, 1939		
Orry-Kelly born, 1897			Ray Milland born, 1905
8:00	8:00	8:00	8:00
9:00	9:00	9:00	9:00
10:00	10:00	10:00	10:00
11:00	11:00	11:00	11:00
Noon	Noon	Noon	Noon
1:00	1:00	1:00	1:00
2:00	2:00	2:00	2:00
3:00	3:00	3:00	3:00
4:00	4:00	4:00	4:00
5:00	5:00	5:00	5:00
6:00	6:00	6:00	6:00
7:00	7:00	7:00	7:00

FRIDAY

4

8:00

9:00

10:00

11:00

Noon

1:00

2:00

3:00

4:00

5:00

6:00

7:00

SATURDAY

5

SUNDAY

6

Loretta Young born, 1913

Loretta Young born, January 6, 1913 (*The Men in Her Life*, with Conrad Veidt)

ALMANAC

Note: Where specific dates or sites are not listed, information was not available at press time.

1984 AWARDS

Golden Globe Awards	January 28
New York Film Critics Awards	January 29
Iris Awards	February
AFI Life Achievement Award	March
Writers Guild Awards	March or April
Academy Awards	March or April
Directors Guild of America Awards	March 10
Council of International Nontheatrical Events (CINE) Gold Eagle Competition	April & September
Academy of Motion Picture Arts & Sciences Student Film Awards	June
Clio Awards	June 13
Emmy Awards	September

1984 FESTIVALS

New York Independent Film Makers Exposition	January 28-29
Berlin Film Festival	February
U.S.A. Film Festival (Dallas)	Spring
Cannes Film Festival	May
American Film Festival (New York)	May
Venice Film Festival	Summer
Sinking Creek (Tennessee) Film Celebration	June
Los Angeles International Film Exposition	August 19-September 8
Telluride Film Festival	August 31-September 3
New York Film Festival	September
International Film and Television Festival of New York	October 31-November 2
London Film Festival	November
Chicago International Film Festival	November 4-18

1984 MEETINGS, CONVENTIONS

National Association of Television Programming Executives Conference	February 10-14 San Francisco
Society for Cinema Studies Annual Conference	March 29-April 1 Madison, Wisconsin
International Federation of Film Archives Annual Meeting	April 5-11 Stockholm
Broadcast Education Association Annual Convention	April 27-28 Las Vegas
MIP-TV International Programming Market	April 27-May 3 Cannes
National Association of Broadcasters Annual Convention	April 29-May 2 Las Vegas
American Women in Radio and Television Annual Convention	May 30-June 2 Chicago
National Cable Television Association Annual Convention	June 3-6 Las Vegas
University Film and Video Association Convention	August
National Association of Theatre Owners Convention	October 30-November 4 Washington, D.C.
Society of Motion Picture and Television Engineers Convention	October 27-November 3 New York

1983 ACADEMY AWARDS

Best Picture: *Gandhi*

Best Foreign Language Film: *To Begin Again*

Best Director: Richard Attenborough, for *Gandhi*

Best Actor: Ben Kingsley, for *Gandhi*

Best Actress: Meryl Streep, for *Sophie's Choice*

Best Supporting Actor: Louis Gossett, Jr., for *An Officer and a Gentleman*

Best Supporting Actress: Jessica Lange, for *Tootsie*

Best Original Screenplay: John Briley, for *Gandhi*

Best Adapted Screenplay: Costa-Gavras and Donald Stewart, for *Missing*

Best Best Cinematography: Billy Williams and Ronnie Taylor, for *Gandhi*

Best Editing: John Bloom, for *Gandhi*

Best Art Direction: Stuart Craig and Bob Laing; Michael Seirton, set decoration, for *Gandhi*

Best Visual Effects: Carlo Rambaldi, Dennis Murren, and Kenneth Smith, for *E.T.*

Best Costume Design: John Mollo and Bhanu Athaiya, for *Gandhi*

Best Sound: Buzz Knudson, Robert Glass, Don Digirolamo, and Gene Cantamessa, for *E.T.*

Best Sound Effects Editing: Charles L. Campbell, Ben Burtt, for *E.T.*

Best Makeup: Sarah Monzani and Michele Burke, for *Quest for Fire*

Best Original Song: "Up Where We Belong;" music by Jack Nitzsche and Buffy Sainte-Marie, lyrics by Wil Jennings, for *An Officer and a Gentleman*

Best Original Score: John Williams, for *E.T.*

Best Adapted Score: Henry Mancini, Leslie Bricusse, for *Victor/Victoria*

Best Documentary Feature: *Just Another Missing Kid*

Best Documentary Short: *If You Love This Planet*

Best Live-Action Short: *A Shocking Accident*

Best Animated Short: *Tango*

TOP-RATED TELEVISION SERIES, 1982-1983 SEASON

1. "60 Minutes"
2. "Dallas"
3. (tie) "M*A*S*H"
   "Magnum, P.I."
5. "Dynasty"
6. "Three's Company"
7. "Simon & Simon"
8. "Falcon Crest"
8. "Love Boat"
10. (tie) "The A Team"
    "NFL Monday Night Football"
12. (tie) "The Jeffersons"
    "Newhart"
14. (tie) "Fall Guy"
    "The Mississippi"
16. "9 to 5"
17. "One Day at a Time"
18. "Hart to Hart"
19. (tie) "Gloria"
    "Trapper John, M.D."
    "Goodnight, Beantown"
22. "Knots Landing"
23. (tie) "Hill Street Blues"
    "Ryan's Four"
25. (tie) "That's Incredible"
    "Archie Bunker's Place"

FOR FURTHER INFORMATION . . .

A selected list of sources of information on film and television.
(NOTE: A local public library may be the first place to turn for help.)

Academy of Motion Picture Arts
and Sciences
The Margaret Herrick Library
8949 Wilshire Blvd.
Beverly Hills, CA 90211 (213) 278-4313
(Books, periodicals, clippings file, stills
collection.)
National Film Information Service at same
address offers mail access to library holdings.

The American Film Institute
Louis B. Mayer Library
2021 N. Western Ave.
P.O. Box 27999
Los Angeles, CA 90027 (213) 856-7655
(Books, periodicals, clippings files. Transcripts
of AFI seminars and oral histories.)

The American Film Institute
Resource Center
J. F. Kennedy Center
Washington, DC 20566 (202) 828-4088
(Books, periodicals, clippings files.)

Billy Rose Theatre Collection
111 Amsterdam Ave.
New York, NY 10023 (212) 870-1639
(Books, periodicals, clippings files, archival
collection, stills.)

Broadcast Pioneers Library
1771 N St., N.W.
Washington, DC 20036 (202) 223-0088
(Primary materials on history of broadcasting.)

Donnell Media Center Library
20 West 53rd St.
New York, NY 10019 (212) 621-0609
(Viewing facilities for film and video; vertical
files of study guides to film/video collection and
subject files.)

Education Film Library Association
43 West 61st St.
New York, NY 10023 (212) 246-4533
(Subject and title files on educational and
16mm films and videotapes.)

Federal Communications Commission Library
1919 M St., N.W. Room 639
Washington, DC 20554 (202) 632-7100
(Books, periodicals, files on broadcasting.)

Library of Congress
Motion Pictures, Broadcasting, and Recorded
Sound Division
Washington, DC 20540 (202) 287-1000
(Books, periodicals, film collection, videotapes
available for viewing by serious scholars.)

Museum of Broadcasting
1 East 53rd St.
New York, NY 10022 (212) 752-4690
(Television programs and scripts.)

Museum of Modern Art
Film Study Center
11 West 53rd St.
New York, NY 10019
(Clippings files, archives materials, viewing
service.)
Note: Because of construction, collection is now
located at 18 W. 54th St., New York, NY
10019. (212) 708-9613. Mailing address
remains as above.

National Archives and Records Service
Special Archives Division
8th St. & Pennsylvania Ave., N.W.
Washington, DC 20408
(202) 523-3236 (Still Picture Branch)
(202) 786-0041 (Motion Picture and Sound
Recording Branch)
(Stills collection, government-produced film
collection, viewing facilities.)

National Association of Broadcasters Library
1771 N St., N.W.
Washington, DC 20036 (202) 293-3579
(Books and periodicals.)

Northwest Film Study Center
Portland Art Association
1219 S.W. Park Ave.
Portland, OR 97205 (503) 221-1156
(Books, periodicals, clippings files, stills
collection, viewing facilities, circulating film
library, exhibition program, and classes.)

Pacific Film Archive
University Art Museum
2625 Durant Ave.
Berkeley, CA (415) 642-1437
(Clippings files, poster and stills collection,
books, periodicals, information files and film
collection.)

Television Information Office Library
745 Fifth Avenue
New York, NY 10151 (212) 759-6800
(Books, periodicals, clippings files on television
only.)

Television News Study Center
The Gelman Library
George Washington University
2130 H St., N.W.
Washington, DC 20052 (202) 676-7218
(Books, periodicals, viewing facilities for
newscast videotapes ordered through the
Vanderbilt Television News Service.)

University Film Study Center
18 Vassar St., Room 20B-120
Massachusetts Institute of Technology
Cambridge, MA 02139 (617) 253-7612
(Books, periodicals, clippings files.)

University of California-Los Angeles
Theater Arts Library
Los Angeles, CA 90024 (213) 825-4880
(Books, periodicals, clippings files, stills
collection, scripts, oral histories, production
materials.)

University of Southern California
Department of Special Collections
Doheny Library
University Park
Los Angeles, CA 90089-0182 (213) 743-6058
(Books, periodicals, archival collection, scripts
and stills collections, viewing facilities,
audio and videotapes.)

Vanderbilt Television News Archive
Joint University Libraries
Nashville, TN 37240-0007 (615) 322-2927
(Viewing facilities for videotaped newscasts
from August 1968 to present.)

Wisconsin Center for Film and Theater
Research
Film Archive
816 State St.
Madison, WI 53706 (608) 262-0585
(Films, scripts and documentation, stills
collection, periodicals, books, viewing facilities.)

IMPORTANT ADDRESSES/TELEPHONE NUMBERS

1983

JANUARY
S	M	T	W	T	F	S
						1
2	3	4	5	6	7	8
9	10	11	12	13	14	15
16	17	18	19	20	21	22
23	24	25	26	27	28	29
30	31					

FEBRUARY
S	M	T	W	T	F	S
		1	2	3	4	5
6	7	8	9	10	11	12
13	14	15	16	17	18	19
20	21	22	23	24	25	26
27	28					

MARCH
S	M	T	W	T	F	S
		1	2	3	4	5
6	7	8	9	10	11	12
13	14	15	16	17	18	19
20	21	22	23	24	25	26
27	28	29	30	31		

APRIL
S	M	T	W	T	F	S
					1	2
3	4	5	6	7	8	9
10	11	12	13	14	15	16
17	18	19	20	21	22	23
24	25	26	27	28	29	30

MAY
S	M	T	W	T	F	S
1	2	3	4	5	6	7
8	9	10	11	12	13	14
15	16	17	18	19	20	21
22	23	24	25	26	27	28
29	30	31				

JUNE
S	M	T	W	T	F	S
			1	2	3	4
5	6	7	8	9	10	11
12	13	14	15	16	17	18
19	20	21	22	23	24	25
26	27	28	29	30		

JULY
S	M	T	W	T	F	S
					1	2
3	4	5	6	7	8	9
10	11	12	13	14	15	16
17	18	19	20	21	22	23
24	25	26	27	28	29	30
31						

AUGUST
S	M	T	W	T	F	S
	1	2	3	4	5	6
7	8	9	10	11	12	13
14	15	16	17	18	19	20
21	22	23	24	25	26	27
28	29	30	31			

SEPTEMBER
S	M	T	W	T	F	S
				1	2	3
4	5	6	7	8	9	10
11	12	13	14	15	16	17
18	19	20	21	22	23	24
25	26	27	28	29	30	

OCTOBER
S	M	T	W	T	F	S
						1
2	3	4	5	6	7	8
9	10	11	12	13	14	15
16	17	18	19	20	21	22
23	24	25	26	27	28	29
30	31					

NOVEMBER
S	M	T	W	T	F	S
		1	2	3	4	5
6	7	8	9	10	11	12
13	14	15	16	17	18	19
20	21	22	23	24	25	26
27	28	29	30			

DECEMBER
S	M	T	W	T	F	S
				1	2	3
4	5	6	7	8	9	10
11	12	13	14	15	16	17
18	19	20	21	22	23	24
25	26	27	28	29	30	31

1984

JANUARY
S	M	T	W	T	F	S
1	2	3	4	5	6	7
8	9	10	11	12	13	14
15	16	17	18	19	20	21
22	23	24	25	26	27	28
29	30	31				

FEBRUARY
S	M	T	W	T	F	S
			1	2	3	4
5	6	7	8	9	10	11
12	13	14	15	16	17	18
19	20	21	22	23	24	25
26	27	28	29			

MARCH
S	M	T	W	T	F	S
				1	2	3
4	5	6	7	8	9	10
11	12	13	14	15	16	17
18	19	20	21	22	23	24
25	26	27	28	29	30	31

APRIL
S	M	T	W	T	F	S
1	2	3	4	5	6	7
8	9	10	11	12	13	14
15	16	17	18	19	20	21
22	23	24	25	26	27	28
29	30					

MAY
S	M	T	W	T	F	S
		1	2	3	4	5
6	7	8	9	10	11	12
13	14	15	16	17	18	19
20	21	22	23	24	25	26
27	28	29	30	31		

JUNE
S	M	T	W	T	F	S
					1	2
3	4	5	6	7	8	9
10	11	12	13	14	15	16
17	18	19	20	21	22	23
24	25	26	27	28	29	30

JULY
S	M	T	W	T	F	S
1	2	3	4	5	6	7
8	9	10	11	12	13	14
15	16	17	18	19	20	21
22	23	24	25	26	27	28
29	30	31				

AUGUST
S	M	T	W	T	F	S
			1	2	3	4
5	6	7	8	9	10	11
12	13	14	15	16	17	18
19	20	21	22	23	24	25
26	27	28	29	30	31	

SEPTEMBER
S	M	T	W	T	F	S
						1
2	3	4	5	6	7	8
9	10	11	12	13	14	15
16	17	18	19	20	21	22
23	24	25	26	27	28	29
30						

OCTOBER
S	M	T	W	T	F	S
	1	2	3	4	5	6
7	8	9	10	11	12	13
14	15	16	17	18	19	20
21	22	23	24	25	26	27
28	29	30	31			

NOVEMBER
S	M	T	W	T	F	S
				1	2	3
4	5	6	7	8	9	10
11	12	13	14	15	16	17
18	19	20	21	22	23	24
25	26	27	28	29	30	

DECEMBER
S	M	T	W	T	F	S
						1
2	3	4	5	6	7	8
9	10	11	12	13	14	15
16	17	18	19	20	21	22
23	24	25	26	27	28	29
30	31					

1985

JANUARY
S	M	T	W	T	F	S
		1	2	3	4	5
6	7	8	9	10	11	12
13	14	15	16	17	18	19
20	21	22	23	24	25	26
27	28	29	30	31		

FEBRUARY
S	M	T	W	T	F	S
					1	2
3	4	5	6	7	8	9
10	11	12	13	14	15	16
17	18	19	20	21	22	23
24	25	26	27	28		

MARCH
S	M	T	W	T	F	S
					1	2
3	4	5	6	7	8	9
10	11	12	13	14	15	16
17	18	19	20	21	22	23
24	25	26	27	28	29	30
31						

APRIL
S	M	T	W	T	F	S
	1	2	3	4	5	6
7	8	9	10	11	12	13
14	15	16	17	18	19	20
21	22	23	24	25	26	27
28	29	30				

MAY
S	M	T	W	T	F	S
			1	2	3	4
5	6	7	8	9	10	11
12	13	14	15	16	17	18
19	20	21	22	23	24	25
26	27	28	29	30	31	

JUNE
S	M	T	W	T	F	S
						1
2	3	4	5	6	7	8
9	10	11	12	13	14	15
16	17	18	19	20	21	22
23	24	25	26	27	28	29
30						

JULY
S	M	T	W	T	F	S
	1	2	3	4	5	6
7	8	9	10	11	12	13
14	15	16	17	18	19	20
21	22	23	24	25	26	27
28	29	30	31			

AUGUST
S	M	T	W	T	F	S
				1	2	3
4	5	6	7	8	9	10
11	12	13	14	15	16	17
18	19	20	21	22	23	24
25	26	27	28	29	30	31

SEPTEMBER
S	M	T	W	T	F	S
1	2	3	4	5	6	7
8	9	10	11	12	13	14
15	16	17	18	19	20	21
22	23	24	25	26	27	28
29	30					

OCTOBER
S	M	T	W	T	F	S
		1	2	3	4	5
6	7	8	9	10	11	12
13	14	15	16	17	18	19
20	21	22	23	24	25	26
27	28	29	30	31		

NOVEMBER
S	M	T	W	T	F	S
					1	2
3	4	5	6	7	8	9
10	11	12	13	14	15	16
17	18	19	20	21	22	23
24	25	26	27	28	29	30

DECEMBER
S	M	T	W	T	F	S
1	2	3	4	5	6	7
8	9	10	11	12	13	14
15	16	17	18	19	20	21
22	23	24	25	26	27	28
29	30	31				